Diagnostizieren & Fördern

Ein Kernanliegen von Schule ist es, für jede Schülerin und jeden Schüler ein **individuelles Leistungsprofil** zu erstellen und jeden Jugendlichen entsprechend seinen Möglichkeiten zu fordern bzw. zu fördern.
Schriftliche Leistungsüberprüfungen, Lernstandserhebungen u. Ä. können Aufschluss geben, reichen aber nicht aus, um ein dezidiertes Leistungsprofil einer Schülerin oder eines Schülers zu erstellen. Dazu müssen unterschiedliche Ebenen beachtet werden:

Ebene I	Ebene II	Ebene III
Persönlichkeit	Lebens- und Schulsituation	Englischunterricht

Ebene I: Persönlichkeit
- Allgemeines Leistungsvermögen:
  Lernbereitschaft, Merkfähigkeit ...
- Arbeitsverhalten:
  Belastbarkeit, Konzentrationsfähigkeit, Aufmerksamkeitsstörungen ...
- Soziales Verhalten
  Fähigkeit zur Kooperation, aggressives Verhalten ...
- Beziehung zur Lehrperson:
  positive oder negative Grundhaltung
- Individuelle Interessen und Neigungen

Ebene II: Lebens- und Schulsituation
- Allgemeine Lebenssituation:
  behütendes Elternhaus, besondere familiäre Belastungen ...
- Schulische Situation:
  schulische Entwicklung

Ebene III: Unterricht
- Subjektive Einstellung zum Schulfach
- Leistungsbereitschaft
- Beherrschung fachlicher Inhalte, Begriffe und Methoden
- Verwendung von Medien
- Fähigkeit, fachliche Sachverhalte zu verstehen und Verstandenes zu nutzen
- Fähigkeit, fachliche Sachverhalte zu kommunizieren und verständlich zu argumentieren.

Die Ebenen I und II lassen sich naturgemäß durch die Schule nur bedingt beeinflussen. Die vorliegenden Materialien unterstützen die Arbeit in Bezug auf die Ebene III.

Hinweise zum Einsatz der Materialien

Das vorliegende Themenheft *Diagnostizieren und Fördern Englisch 7./8. Schuljahr* ist einsetzbar in speziellen Förderstunden, im Unterricht oder auch zur häuslichen Übung. Sämtliche Arbeitsblätter sind so gestaltet, dass Schülerinnen und Schüler ohne weitere Erläuterungen mit ihnen arbeiten können. Es sollte aber in jedem Fall **Ansprechpartner** zur Klärung von Lernwegen geben. Dies können Lehrer, Schüler höherer Klassen oder andere Mentoren sein. Ihre Funktion besteht zum einen darin, bestimmte Teile der Lösungen zu kontrollieren (offene und halb-offene Aufgabenformate, geschlossene Aufgaben können dagegen auch von Mitschülern korrigiert werden). Zum anderen sollten die Mentoren auf der Grundlage der bearbeiteten Materialien so oft wie möglich mit einzelnen Schülerinnen und Schülern kurze Beratungsgespräche führen, um Rückmeldungen über bereits erreichte Kompetenzen zu geben und fehlerhaft gelöste Aufgaben gemeinsam zu analysieren und zu reflektieren. Auf diese Weise werden für den Schüler oder die Schülerin Fehler verstehbar, und neue kognitive Herangehensweisen an Problemstellungen können angebahnt werden.
Im Themenheft erfolgt eine Fokussierung auf fachliche **Schwerpunktthemen** des Doppeljahrgangs. In diesem Themenheft werden zwei zentrale Lernbereiche des Englischunterrichts der Stufen 7 und 8 angeboten:
① Reading
② Writing

Zu jedem Schwerpunktthema gibt es folgende Materialien:
1. Eine **Lernstandsermittlung**, die einen vertiefenden Blick auf fachliche Fähigkeiten erlaubt und mögliche Stärken und Probleme aufdeckt. Im Zuge der **Auswertung der Lernstandsermittlung** werden Hinweise darauf gegeben, mit welchem Fördermaterial gearbeitet werden sollte.
2. **Fördermaterial** für unterschiedliche Kompetenzstufen, das ein selbstständiges Arbeiten und Üben ermöglicht.
3. Eine auf die erste Lernstandsermittlung rückbezogene **Lernfortschrittsermittlung**, die Schlüsse darauf zulässt, in welchem Maße sich Fähigkeiten weiterentwickelt haben.

1. Lernstandsermittlung und Fehleranalyse

Schwächen, die Kinder und Jugendliche in der Auseinandersetzung mit Problemstellungen zeigen, sind nicht unbedingt als etwas Negatives zu bewerten, sie können auch als Grundlage für die Erarbeitung objektiv korrekter Lösungsstrategien dienen. Fehler zeigen meist, an welchem Punkt sich ein Lernender zurzeit befindet und welche fachlichen Hilfsmittel ihm momentan zur Lösung eines Problems zur Verfügung stehen. Um fehlerhafte Denkstrategien aufzuschlüsseln, ist es hilfreich, sich in diese einzudenken.

Besonders aufschlussreich ist dazu die **prozessbegleitende Fehleranalyse**, bei der Schülerinnen und Schüler ihre Denkprozesse erläutern. Dies kann entweder durch mündliche oder durch schriftliche Erklärungen erfolgen. Die prozessbegleitende Fehleranalyse durch mündliche Erläuterungen eignet sich insbesondere für den (Förder-)Unterricht mit sehr kleinen Lerngruppen oder den Einzelunterricht, denn sie ist sehr zeitaufwändig und erfordert die vollkommene Zuwendung einer Person. Schriftliche Verfahrensweisen, z. B. mit Hilfe von Lerntagebüchern, können auch in größeren Gruppen sinnvoll eingesetzt werden.

Bei der **ergebnisorientierten Fehleranalyse** werden Fehler in Schülerarbeiten (z. B. Übungs- oder Hausaufgaben) auf Gesetzmäßigkeiten überprüft. Erfahrene Lehrkräfte sehen häufig schnell an der Art des Fehlers, welche Strategie zugrunde lag, und können mit den Jugendlichen gemeinsam gezielt an der entsprechenden Stelle weiterarbeiten.

Die **Lernstandsermittlungen** dieses Heftes unterstützen sowohl die Lehrkräfte als auch die Schüler bei der Fehleranalyse, indem sie durch gezielte Aufgabenstellungen bestimmte systematische Fehler im Sinne einer ergebnisorientierten Fehleranalyse herausfordern.

Das Material sollte ohne Notendruck und ohne zeitliche Beschränkung eingesetzt werden.

In den Lernstandsermittlungen wird ein breites Spektrum an Kompetenzebenen abgebildet. Die Ergebnisse der Auswertungen haben Hinweischarakter auf mögliche Kompetenzen und Schwächen von Schülerinnen und Schülern. Aufgrund der jeweiligen Rahmenbedingungen am Testtag (Schülerin X / Schüler Y kann sich an diesem Tag schlecht konzentrieren, eine Aufgabenstellung wird missverstanden ...) können Einzelergebnisse jedoch beeinflusst werden. Deshalb ist es bei Auffälligkeiten empfehlenswert, unterstützend weitere Aufgaben zur Einschätzung einzusetzen, welche sich auf die gleiche Kompetenzebene beziehen. Grundsätzlich gilt: Je mehr Aufgaben zu einer Kompetenzebene durchgearbeitet und analysiert werden, desto sicherer ist auch die Diagnose.

Die Materialien gehen davon aus, dass die Kompetenzen weitgehend hierarchisch aufgebaut sind, höhere Kompetenzstufen in der Regel komplexere Fähigkeiten umfassen. Leistungen einer höheren Kompetenzebene können von Schülerinnen und Schülern gleichwohl auch dann erbracht werden, wenn die vorherige Stufe noch nicht vollständig gesichert ist. Mit dem Diagnosematerial lassen sich Hinweise auf Kompetenzschwerpunkte erhalten.

Die **Auswertung der Lernstandsermittlungen** sollte möglichst zeitnah erfolgen. Bei geschlossenen Aufgaben ist es möglich, die Schülerinnen und Schüler während der Nachbesprechung wechselseitig korrigieren zu lassen, weil in diesem Fall lediglich zwischen richtig und falsch unterschieden werden muss.

2. Fördermaterial

Die sich aus der Lernstandsermittlung ergebenden Förderschwerpunkte sollten mit dem Jugendlichen **besprochen** werden, damit er den folgenden Lernweg reflektiert beschreiten kann. Nur so werden Schülerinnen und Schüler auch willens sein, sich ernsthaft mit den Materialien auseinanderzusetzen und Anstrengungsbereitschaft zu zeigen.

Für jeden Lernbereich gibt es **gestuftes Übungsmaterial**. Je nach Ergebnis der Lernstandsermittlung arbeitet der Jugendliche mit dem Material aus Übungsbereich 1, 2 oder 3.

Für die Übungen eines Übungsbereiches müssten 1 bis 2 Stunden Zeit zur Verfügung stehen, wobei mehrere kleine Pausen einzuplanen sind. Jugendliche, die am gleichen Übungsmaterial arbeiten, sollten die Gelegenheit bekommen, sich zwischendurch über ihre Strategien auszutauschen.

Das im Heft angebotene Übungsmaterial hat **exemplarischen Charakter**, es stellt kein vollständiges Förderprogramm dar. Um eine intensive Förderung zu gewährleisten, muss das Material durch ähnlich gestaltete Übungen ergänzt werden.

Die Übungsmaterialien sind als **Lernaufgaben**, nicht als Überprüfungsaufgaben (z. B. für Klassenarbeiten) gestaltet.

3. Lernfortschrittsermittlung

Am Ende des Kapitels zu einem Lernbereich findet sich eine Lernfortschrittsermittlung, die eingesetzt werden sollte, wenn der Jugendliche das vorhandene und weiteres Übungsmaterial seines Kompetenzprofils bearbeitet hat. Hierbei handelt es sich nicht um eine geeichte Messung des Lernfortschritts, sondern die Lernfortschrittsermittlung soll lediglich Anhaltspunkte liefern, ob weitere Übungen des jeweiligen Schwerpunktes eingesetzt werden müssen oder ein weiterer, komplexerer Übungsbereich angegangen werden kann.

Das Material

In den beiden Lernbereichen dieses Themenheftes stehen jeweils Aspekte im Mittelpunkt, die für den Kompetenzaufbau in den Jahrgangsstufen 7 und 8 zentral sind.

Reading

Die Materialien für den Bereich Leseverstehen können von den Schülerinnen und Schülern weitgehend selbstständig erarbeitet werden, da es sich größtenteils um geschlossene Aufgabenformate handelt.
Die Test- und Übungsmaterialien dieses Kapitels untersuchen und fördern die Fähigkeiten der Schüler zur Informationsentnahme aus englischen Texten.
In der Lernstandsermittlung zu Beginn des Kapitels wird geprüft, inwieweit der Schüler bzw. die Schülerin in der Lage ist,

- einzelne, nicht verschlüsselte Informationen zu lokalisieren und auszuwerten,
- verschlüsselte Informationen zu finden und auszuwerten,
- Beziehungen zwischen Informationen herzustellen oder einen Transfer zu leisten.

In allen drei Übungsbereichen erschließen sich die Schülerinnen und Schüler mithilfe von Vorübungen und der gezielten, schrittweisen Bearbeitung von Verständnisfragen einen neuen Text und verbessern so ihre Lesekompetenz. In einem Zwischencheck werden die Schüler dazu angehalten, ihr Vorgehen zu reflektieren und die erlernte Methode zu verinnerlichen.
Thematisch sind alle Texte dieses Kapitels in den USA angesiedelt: In den Übungsbereichen 1 und 2 handeln die Lesetexte von alltäglichen Erlebnissen und Problemen, die dem Erfahrungshorizont von Schülern und Schülerinnen der 7. und 8. Klasse entsprechen. In den Texten des Übungsbereichs 3 geht es um die US-amerikanischen Nationalparks.

Writing

Die Test-, Auswertungs- und Fördermaterialien dieses Kapitels sind in zwei Themen untergliedert:

- Report
- Biography

Diese können nacheinander oder unabhängig voneinander bearbeitet werden.
In beiden Teilen des Kapitels steht das Verfassen von einfachen englischen Texten (Berichten bzw. Biografien) im Mittelpunkt. Dabei werden sowohl die inhaltliche Textgestaltung (Vollständigkeit, Richtigkeit, Eigenständigkeit, Adressatenorientierung, Textformat) als auch die sprachliche Leistung (Wortschatz, Grammatik und Orthografie) berücksichtigt.
Die Auswertung der Lernstandsermittlung muss durch die Lehrkraft oder einen Mentor erfolgen, da die Kompetenzen anhand eines von dem Schüler oder der Schülerin verfassten Textes ermittelt werden.
Die Übungsmaterialien beider Themenbereiche weisen abhängig vom Kompetenzniveau engere oder weitere Hilfsstrukturen auf und gliedern sich jeweils in einen inhaltlichen und einen sprachlichen Teil.
Im inhaltlichen Teil des Themenbereichs „Report" lernen die Schülerinnen und Schüler, den Aufbau von Berichten (beispielsweise über Sportereignisse oder Unfälle) zu erkennen bzw. selbst umzusetzen. Der sprachliche Teil gliedert sich in Aufgaben zur Erweiterung des textsortenspezifischen Wortschatzes sowie Übungen zum *simple past* und zur Wortstellung in englischen Sätzen.
Im Themenbereich „Biography" üben die Schülerinnen und Schüler, kurze Texte über das Leben bekannter Persönlichkeiten zu verfassen. Im inhaltlichen Teil lernen sie, Informationen zu sammeln und anzuordnen sowie ihren Text sinnvoll zu gliedern. Im sprachlichen Teil stehen die Wortschatzarbeit sowie das Finden und Analysieren von Rechtschreib- und Grammatikfehlern im Mittelpunkt. Außerdem lernen die Schülerinnen und Schüler, Sätze durch *linking words* miteinander zu verknüpfen – ein wichtiger Schritt, wenn es darum geht, flüssige, gut lesbare Texte zu schreiben.

Name: ______________________________ Class: __________ Date: ______________

Lies den folgenden Text mehrfach gründlich durch und beantworte dann die Fragen.

The rock concert

Maureen Donovan had often visited Manhattan with her parents, of course, but she had never been there without them before. So she was very excited when the chance came one day.

My friend Sally had got two tickets for a rock concert from her sister. I almost died when she asked me on the school bus, "Do you want to come with me?" I jumped up and down and shouted, "YES! YES!" until the bus driver said, "Sit down." A rock concert in the city! But inside I began to think: what will my parents say? The rest of the day at school I thought about how I should ask them.

When I got home after school, I said, "Sally has two tickets for the Bruce West concert in Manhattan this weekend. I don't suppose I can go with her?" My mother laughed and said, "That's right. Do you know how old you are?"

"But Mom, please. Sally's sister lives there. She is old enough to go with us. And we could spend the night with her, so you and Dad don't have to worry. And I promise I'll call you after the concert and report what it was like."

Mom thought about it and then smiled. "OK." But she suggested that I should ask Dad, too. I said "Great!" and while I was doing my homework, I thought, "I hope Dad will react the same way."

But when he came through the door, my heart sank. He looked tired and angry. Dad works in Manhattan, so he has to travel there every day. Mom's office is in Brooklyn, so she's usually home much earlier.

Dad threw himself on the sofa and said, "I hate those subways. First an empty train goes past and doesn't stop. Then you wait and wait until another train comes. But it's so full of people that you have to fight to get in. And they're so dirty." Mom said, "I think Maureen wants to ask you something." Dad sat down and said, "Can't it wait till after dinner?"

During the meal Mom and Dad talked about work. It wasn't very interesting, but I sat there quietly and waited. Then Dad talked with my brother about basketball. My brother Scott is already 5 feet 9 inches tall and he's only 13. He wants to get onto the school team this year.

So I waited until they had finished. Then Dad started to help Mom to put away the dishes and clean the kitchen. That was too much. So I told him everything and he just smiled and said, "OK." I couldn't believe my ears.

"But you'll have to be careful, you know. Don't talk to strangers on the subway at night and don't get in if it's empty. Somebody might try to rob you. A lot of those kids carry weapons." I said, "OK." Later I called Sally and told her the good news.

The concert was Friday night and we were so excited as we rode into Manhattan, our first trip there alone. Dad was right about the subway train. It wasn't so crowded on our way into the city, but it was dirty, we couldn't see out. At one station a gang of kids got in and we became a bit nervous. We were afraid that they might attack us. I remembered Dad's words and we sat still and never moved. They looked at us, but then they played music and laughed and danced.

We got off at Spring Street, not far from the place where Sally's sister Jody lives. From there it was a five-minute walk to Jody's apartment in Greenwich Village. It was already six, so Jody suggested we should eat in Chinatown. The walk was about 20 minutes and we had to go though narrow little streets to get there. We went into a small restaurant where everybody, it seemed, was Chinese. "Hey, we're the only Americans," I said. But then Jody said that these were Americans, too. She is right, of course. I couldn't believe that these people could spend their whole lives in a country and perhaps never leave Chinatown. But I could understand that. I feel a lot safer in areas that I know well.

After the meal we caught a cab, and soon we were driving up Broadway towards Madison Square Garden. When we arrived at the Garden, there were already thousands of people outside. They finally opened the doors at eight o'clock. I almost died when everybody tried to get in. We fought the crowds and got great seats at the front, where we had a fantastic view of Bruce and the band. When he appeared everybody shouted and screamed. Then they played one great song after another. It was wonderful. He sang all my favourite songs. At the end of the concert I was almost crazy!

The next day we got up early, and after breakfast we went for a walk around the Village. With its narrow streets and small houses, the Village is very quiet and peaceful. In Washington Square we listened to a group of street musicians. We started to talk to them, and as the weather was so nice, we all went to Central Park together. Both Sally and I felt we were in a different world. All around us was the big busy city with the traffic, noise and skyscrapers, but here in Central Park it was so quiet: people were lying on the grass, jogging, fishing or simply enjoying themselves. We had a wonderful time. Then we looked at the famous stores along Fifth Avenue, and in the afternoon we went back to Brooklyn. When we got off the subway, both of us thought the same thing: How soon can we do this again? (aus: English G A4, Cornelsen, Berlin 1988, pp. 20 – 22)

Working with the text

1. According to Maureen's father: why is it dangerous to go by subway at night?
- ☐ **a)** The subway trains are dirty.
- ☐ **b)** Kids with weapons might rob passengers when they are alone on the train.
- ☐ **c)** The subway trains are always late.
- ☐ **d)** The empty trains do not stop.

2. Where did Sally and Maureen sleep in Manhattan?
- ☐ **a)** In Central Park on the grass.
- ☐ **b)** At Sally's sister's.
- ☐ **c)** At a youth hostel.
- ☐ **d)** They go home at night.

3. How did the girls get to Madison Square Garden?
- ☐ **a)** By train.
- ☐ **b)** By cab.
- ☐ **c)** By bike.
- ☐ **d)** They walk.

4. Why is Central Park special for Sally and Maureen?
- ☐ **a)** There are a lot of expensive shops.
- ☐ **b)** They do not feel like being in a big city because it is quiet there.
- ☐ **c)** The park is in Brooklyn.
- ☐ **d)** They rock concert of Bruce West takes place there.

5. Decide if the following sentences are right or wrong and give the line where you can find this.

	right	wrong	line(s)
a) Maureen is surprised that she is allowed to go to Manhattan with her friend.	☐	☐	______
b) Maureen's father enjoys traveling to work in Manhattan every day.	☐	☐	______
c) Maureen knows Chinatown very well.	☐	☐	______

6. On Saturday after breakfast the girls walked around …
- ☐ **a)** … Chinatown.
- ☐ **b)** … in Brooklyn.
- ☐ **c)** … the streets where Jody lives.
- ☐ **d)** … a little village near New York City.

7. Who went to the rock concert?
- ☐ **a)** Sally, Maureen and the street musicians.
- ☐ **b)** Maureen, Sally and Maureen's sister.
- ☐ **c)** Maureen and Sally.
- ☐ **d)** Maureen, Sally and Jody.

8. Why is it okay for Maureen's mother that her daughter goes to the rock concert in Manhattan?

____

____

9. Why does Maureen's father know the dangers and risks of going to Manhattan by subway?

____

____

10. Where does Maureen live?

____

LÖSUNGEN, FEHLERANALYSE, FÖRDEREMPFEHLUNGEN

Bitte beachten Sie auch die allgemeinen Hinweise am Anfang dieses Themenheftes.

Vorbemerkungen:
Der Text „The rock concert" ist relativ lang, aber von mittlerem Schwierigkeitsgrad. Diese Textlänge ist notwendig, um eine differenzierte Diagnostik zu ermöglichen. Die Testdauer kann je nach Leistungsniveau variieren. Die Testfragen untersuchen die Fähigkeiten der Schülerinnen und Schüler zur Informationsentnahme aus Texten. Die je nach Kompetenzprofil vorgeschlagenen Übungen (siehe Spalte „Förderempfehlung") zielen auf den Erwerb derjenigen Kompetenzen, die im Test nicht zuverlässig gezeigt wurden. Sie sind als Beispielaufgaben zu verstehen, nicht als vollständiges Förderprogramm.

Aufgabe	Lösung	Analyse häufig auftretender Fehler	Förderempfehlung
Nr. 1	Lösung: b	Mehrere Fehler im Bereich der Fragen 1 – 4 weisen darauf hin, dass es dem Schüler/der Schülerin schwerfällt, Informationen zu lokalisieren und dann auszuwerten.	Bei mehreren Fehlern in den Fragen 1 – 4 empfiehlt sich **Übungsbereich** 1. Dort geht es darum, nicht verschlüsselte Informationen zu finden und auszuwerten.
Nr. 2	Lösung: b		
Nr. 3	Lösung: b		
Nr. 4	Lösung: b		
Nr. 5	Lösung: a) right, line 23 b) wrong, lines 13 – 17 c) wrong, lines 34 – 38	Werden die Fragen 1 – 4 recht sicher gelöst, aber im Bereich der Fragen 5 – 6 treten mehrere Fehler auf, so spricht dies dafür, dass der Schüler/die Schülerin zwar Informationen lokalisieren und auswerten kann, es ihm/ihr aber schwerfällt, Informationen auch dann zu lokalisieren und auszuwerten, wenn sie im Text nur in verschlüsselter Form vorliegen.	Bei mehreren Fehlern in den Fragen 5 – 6 empfiehlt sich **Übungsbereich 2.** Dort geht es darum, auch verschlüsselte Informationen zu finden und auszuwerten. Gibt es sowohl in den Fragen 1 – 4 als auch in den Fragen 5 und 6 mehrere Fehler, so sollte mit Übungsbereich 1 begonnen werden, der die fundamentalere Fähigkeit einübt.
Nr. 6	Lösung: c		
Nr. 7	Lösung: d	Werden die Fragen 1 – 5 recht sicher gelöst, aber im Bereich der Fragen 7 – 8 zeigen sich Fehler, so spricht dies dafür, dass es dem Schüler/der Schülerin sehr wohl gelingt, Informationen sogar in verschlüsselter Form zu lokalisieren und auszuwerten, dass es ihm/ihr aber schwerfällt, Beziehungen zwischen Informationen herzustellen oder einen Transfer zu leisten. Das Hauptaugenmerk für die Fragen 8 – 10 liegt auf der inhaltlichen Korrektheit der Lösungen.	Bei Fehlern in den Fragen 7 – 9 empfiehlt sich **Übungsbereich 3.** Gibt es auch in den Fragen 5 – 6 mehrere Fehler, so sollte mit Übungsbereich 2 begonnen werden. Treten zudem Fehler in den Fragen 1 – 4 auf, so sollte Übungsbereich 1 am Anfang stehen.
Nr. 8	Lösung: Sally's older sister will go with the girls. The girls can sleep at Jody's as well.		
Nr. 9	Lösung: Maureen's father works in Manhattan. He goes there by subway probably every day.		
Nr. 10	Lösung: She lives in Brooklyn.		

Hinweis:
Sollte ein Schüler oder eine Schülerin alle zehn Fragen richtig beantworten, so ist seine/ihre Lesekompetenz schon so weit ausgebildet, dass mit dem vorliegenden Material keine Förderung möglich ist.

A dangerous city?

Informationen finden und auswerten

In Übungsbereich 1 übst du, Informationen in einem Text zu finden und sie zur Beantwortung einer Frage zu nutzen.

Vorübungen

1. Antworten zu Fragen finden

Du sollst folgende Frage beantworten:
What exactly is "Ground Zero"?

Dazu findest du unten einen kurzen Text.
Finde die Aussage heraus, die dir hilft, die Frage zu beantworten.

a) Entscheide zunächst, welche Wörter in der Frage wichtig sind:

Wichtige Wörter in der Frage sind: ____________________ und ____________________

b) Suche nun in dem folgenden Text eine Aussage, die die Frage beantwortet, und unterstreiche sie.

9/11 and Ground Zero

On September 11th (9/11), 2001, 19 hijackers took over four US planes. They flew two of them into the Twin Towers of the World Trade Center, in the south of the island of Manhattan. Both skyscrapers burned and collapsed. About 2,750 people died. The place where the Towers stood is now called "Ground Zero". Every year on 9/11 the "Tribute in Light" helps New Yorkers remember the people who died in the two buildings.
(aus: English G 21 A4, Cornelsen, Berlin 2008, S. 17)

c) Nun beantworte die Frage: What exactly is "Ground Zero"?

Antwort: ____

____

2. Informationen in einem Text suchen

Füge Pfeile ein und ergänze die Sätze in der rechten Spalte.

9/11 and Ground Zero

On September 11th (9/11), 2001, 19 hijackers took over four US planes. They flew two of them into the Twin Towers of the World Trade Center, in the south of the island of Manhattan. Both skyscrapers burned and collapsed. About 2,750 people died. The place where the Towers stood is now called "Ground Zero". Every year on 9/11 the "Tribute in Light" helps New Yorkers remember the people who died in the two buildings.

a) Four US planes were taken over by ____________________

____

b) Two planes crashed into ____________________

____

____

c) The Twin Towers were situated ____________________

____

____

d) To remember the victims, every year on 9/11 there is ____________________

____

Übungen zu einem Text

Lies den folgenden Text in vier Schritten:

1. Lesen ohne Bleistift/Textmarker: Überfliege zunächst einmal den Text, um zu sehen, worum es geht.
2. Lesen mit Bleistift/Textmarker: Lies den Text nun gründlich mit einem Bleistift/Textmarker in der Hand. Unterstreiche die Sätze, die wichtige Informationen zu Sven Timmermanns Erlebnissen in der U-Bahn enthalten.
3. Randnotizen: Notiere im dritten Schritt am Rand zu jeder unterstrichenen Stelle einige Stichworte: Was erfährt man an dieser Stelle über Sven Timmermanns Erlebnisse in der U-Bahn?
4. Nach dem Lesen: Lies dir noch einmal deine Stichworte am Rand durch und überlege, was du nun über Sven Timmermanns Erlebnisse in der U-Bahn weißt.

Bearbeite dann die Aufgaben zum Text.

A dangerous city?

When Sven Timmermann opened his eyes, he didn't know where he was. Then he remembered: New York City. The 19-year-old-student had arrived late the night before from Germany. Sven looked at his watch. Eleven o'clock: he had slept much longer than usual. It was too late to go on the guided tour of Manhattan now. Sven had no other plans until that evening, when he planned to go to a jazz concert at Lincoln Center. "Never mind," he thought. "If I have an early lunch, I can walk round the city alone all afternoon." However, the idea made him a bit nervous.

After lunch, Sven left his hotel and walked to the corner of Fifth Avenue. On his left he saw the Empire State building and decided to go there. At first he felt safe with so many people around him. Then he thought he felt something behind him. He put his hand in his pocket; his money was still there.

Sven arrived at the Empire State Building and took the lift to the top. It was a clear day, and he could see all five New York boroughs. Later, he decided to go on his own tour of Manhattan – on foot.

Then, in the early evening, he remembered the jazz concert at Lincoln Center. At the next corner he saw a subway sign: Washington Square (Wash Sq). Sven walked quickly towards it. He asked a man how to get to Lincoln Center. "Change at 42nd Street and get off at 66th." Sven went down to the platform. There was only one person there – a young woman – and she was leaving. She walked past Sven and started to go up the stairs. Suddenly Sven heard something on the stairs behind him. He turned round and saw a young man in a black leather jacket next to the woman.

The man hit the woman and took her bag. Just then a train came into the station. What could Sven do? He was frightened. At the next station two policemen were standing on the platform. "Has the young woman called the police?" Sven thought.

But the policemen didn't do anything. The platform was crowded. The young man got off and disappeared in the crowd. Sven left the train at 42nd Street and changed for 66th Street. When he thought he was at 66th Street he looked out of the window. He couldn't believe it: West 4th Street. He had gotten on the wrong train.

He was back in the area he had just left. Sven became very nervous again and decided to take a bus. He got off the train and ran up to the street.

Outside, it was already dark, and all around him there were empty streets. Then Sven saw a man on the other side of the street. The man could explain to him which bus he had to take. Sven started to cross the street. Just then the man walked under a street light, and Sven saw his black leather jacket. Sven turned round and began to run.

(aus: English G, Vorschläge zur Leistungsmessung Bd. A4, Cornelsen, Berlin 1. Auflage, 4. Druck 1992, S. 14)

Aufgaben zu „A dangerous city?"

1. Who is Sven Timmermann?

a) Die zentralen Wörter in der Frage sind: <u>who</u> und ______________________________.

b) Suche und markiere im Text – mit Textmarker – die Stelle, die zu den zentralen Wörtern der Frage passt.

Diese Stelle passt zur Frage: Zeile(n) ______________________________

c) Beantworte nun die Frage: Sven Timmermann is ______________________________.

2. When did Sven Timmermann arrive in New York?

a) Markiere zunächst mit Textmarker in der Frage alle wichtigen Wörter.

b) Suche und markiere im Text die Stelle, die zu den zentralen Wörtern der Frage passt.

Folgende Stelle gibt Auskunft zu der Frage: Zeile(n) ______________________________

c) Kreuze nun die richtige Antwort an:

He arrived in New York ...

☐ ... the night before. ☐ ... that morning.

☐ ... at 11 o'clock. ☐ ... late in the afternoon.

Zwischencheck: Wie bist du bisher vorgegangen?

In den Aufgaben 1–2 hast du geübt, wie man vorgehen kann, wenn man eine Information sucht.
Schaue dir die zwei Aufgaben nochmals an und ergänze dann:
Wenn ich eine Information suche, um damit eine Antwort zu einer Frage zu finden, dann gehe ich so vor:

Ich beginne wie in Teil (a) der Aufgaben: Zuerst ______________________________

____

Anschließend gehe ich wie in Teil (b) der Aufgaben vor: Ich ______________________________

____

Und schließlich beantworte ich ______________________________

3. Where did Sven plan to go that evening?

a) Schaue auf den Zwischencheck und gehe entsprechend vor.

b) Beantworte nun die Frage:

Sven Timmermann planned to go to ____________________.

c) In the early evening Sven wants to use the subway to get to the jazz concert. Reading the subway map is not easy. Look at the text and find out where Sven starts his journey on the subway. (Schaue wieder auf den Zwischencheck und gehe entsprechend vor!)

Where is Sven?

He is at ______________________________.

Where does he want to go?

He wants to go to ______________________________.

Where does he have to change?

He changes at ______________________________.

Where does he have to get off?

He has to get off at ______________________________

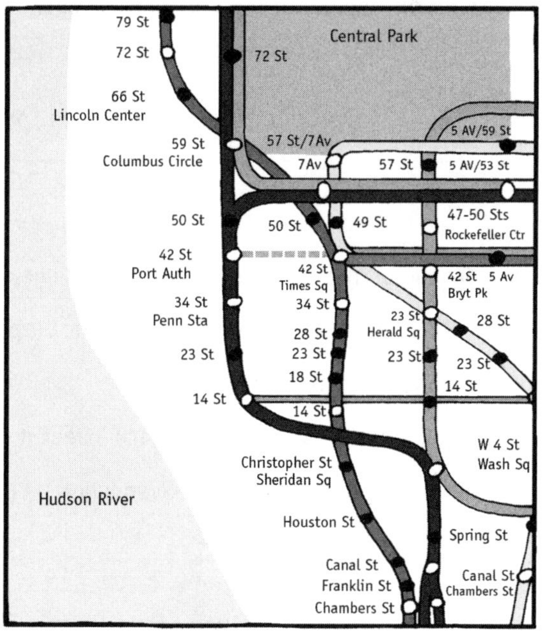

d) Markiere in dem U-Bahn-Plan die Strecke, die er nehmen muss, mit einem Textmarker.

4. Say why Sven didn't finally arrive at 66th Street as he had planned.

a) Markiere in der Frage alle Schlüsselwörter und suche den Textabschnitt, der dazu passt. Markiere auch dort die Schlüsselwörter.

b) Folgender Textabschnitt wurde von mir markiert: Zeile __________________ bis Zeile __________________.

c) Beantworte nun die Frage: Sven Timmermann didn't arrive at 66th Street because ____.

> **Tipp** *Achtung: Die Antwort auf die folgende Frage steht nicht in einem Satz.*

5. Who was the man on the other side of the street?

a) Kreuze die zutreffende Antwort an.
When Sven saw a man on the other side of the street he thought the man was ...

- ☐ ... the man who had stolen his money.
- ☐ ... a policeman.
- ☐ ... the man who had taken the woman's bag.

b) Explain why.

____

____

6. Right or wrong?

Entscheide aufgrund des Textes, ob folgende Aussagen zutreffen, und gib in der rechten Spalte eine Textstelle (Zeile) an, die deine Entscheidung belegt.

> **Tipp** *Du solltest die vorgegebenen Sätze ganz genau mit dem Text vergleichen!*

	right	wrong	line(s)
a) From the corner of 5th Avenue he could see the Lincoln Center.	☐	☐	_____
b) Before Sven took a lift to the top of the Empire State Building, someone stole his money.	☐	☐	_____
c) When Sven got outside at West 4th Street it was already dark.	☐	☐	_____
d) There were people all around Sven when he got out of the subway station.	☐	☐	_____

Leaving Home – Extracts from Maureen's diary

Informationen entschlüsseln und auswerten

In Übungsbereich 2 übst du, Informationen in einem Text auch dann zu finden und auszuwerten, wenn diese im Text anders formuliert sind als in der Frage.

Vorübungen

1. Informationen umformulieren I

Lies die Informationen und ergänze danach die Lücken.

Wenn jemand sagt ...
Mrs Donovan and Mr Donovan are Maureen's parents.
Maureen's ancestors came to the USA from Ireland in 1846.

Dann sagt er damit gleichzeitig:

Mrs Donovan is Maureen's ____________________ and Mr Donovan is Maureen's ____________________.

Maureen's ancestors were ____________________ immigrants.

2. Gleiche Informationen in unterschiedlichem Gewand

Betrachte folgende Sätze:
Maureen Donovan is 14 years old. Her friend is called Sally. Her brother Scott Donovan is 13 years old and he lives with Maureen and their parents in the Big Apple.

Daraus lässt sich mit Sicherheit sagen:

☐ **a)** Sally is 14 years old.
☐ **b)** Maureen and Scott live in New York City.
☐ **c)** Scott is older than his sister.
☐ **d)** Sally's mother is Mexican.

3. Informationen umformulieren II

Vervollständige auf der Grundlage des linken Textes jeweils den rechten Text.

Dieser Text ...	... bedeutet auch:
a) Maureen Donovan's ancestors were Irish immigrants. They came to the USA by ship in 1846. They left Ireland because they suffered from poverty and hunger.	Maureen's ancestors came from ____________________. They left their home country because they were ____________________.
b) Maureen loves vegetables. She is a vegetarian.	Maureen doesn't eat ____________________.

Übungen zu einem Text

Lies den Text auf der nächsten Seite in vier Schritten:

1. Lesen ohne Bleistift/Textmarker: Überfliege zunächst einmal den Text, um zu sehen, worum es geht.
2. Lesen mit Bleistift/Textmarker: Lies den Text nun gründlich mit einem Bleistift/Textmarker in der Hand. Unterstreiche die Sätze, die wichtige Informationen über Maureens Umzug und ihre ersten Tage in Livermore enthalten.
3. Randnotizen: Notiere im dritten Schritt am Rand zu jeder unterstrichenen Stelle einige Stichworte: Was erfährt man an dieser Stelle über Maureens Umzug und ihre ersten Tage in Livermore?
4. Nach dem Lesen: Lies dir noch einmal deine Stichworte am Rand durch und überlege, was du nun über Maureens Umzug und ihre ersten Tage in Livermore weißt.

Bearbeite dann die Aufgaben zum Text.

Leaving home

Maureen Donovan, 14, of New York City, is moving to Livermore, a small city about 40 miles east of San Francisco, with her family – her brother, 13, and her parents. Her parents have both found new jobs in California. Her mother has got a job in a law firm, and her father is going to work as a computer expert with a telephone company in San Francisco. So the whole family has to move. Used to living in a big city, Maureen is shocked by the idea of having to move thousands of miles away to a small place in California. This is what she writes in her diary:

August 10: The big day has finally arrived. We're moving! I said goodbye to my friends today. It was real sad. They were all very sorry. Everybody was so nice to me. Glad nobody saw me cry. Still haven't said goodbye to Sally yet. That won't be easy. She's the best friend I've ever had. I won't find anybody like her in Livermore. One of the guys said I'd die of boredom there.

August 11: The moving van arrived today. Believe it or not, Mom and Dad are really looking forward to moving. I guess it is exciting – for them – like going on vacation. But then I remember we'll never come back. Mom and Dad have decided we're going to drive there. They want us to see what the country is like so we can see that there are nicer places than Brooklyn. I think Brooklyn is fine.

August 15: We're in a motel in Kansas. So far there's been nothing interesting to look at. All I've seen are motels, gas stations and highways. I never dreamed that the trip would last so long. We've been driving for days and we aren't even halfway there. Mom and Dad talk a lot about the trails the early settlers used and said we were following one now. I can't imagine there were once settlers here in their covered wagons and cowboys and Indians.

August 16: Still in Kansas. Another boring day. Dad got mad because he heard me say how boring the trip was. Scott and I sat on the back seat and listened to music while he tried to make us listen to his stupid geography lessons. How can anybody find wheat fields interesting?

August 18: We're in Colorado now and things are getting more interesting. We visited the Rocky Mountain National Park, north of Denver. That was wonderful. Huge mountains and rivers and fields full of flowers. We even visited a gold mine. A miner showed us how to look for gold in the rivers. People still look for gold up here even today, although there's not much to be found.

August 20: Wow! We're crossing Indian land and the scenery is out of this world. And it's so hot. Even I felt nervous when I saw the desert and the rocks – and I was sitting in a car. Dad nearly panicked when he realized we didn't have much gas and the nearest gas station was over 30 miles away. I wonder how the settlers felt when they traveled through here, no water, a hot sun and afraid that Indians might appear any time. It seems strange to see Indians drive cars and sit in restaurants, just like normal Americans.

August 23: Drove through the Navajo reservation to the Grand Canyon. When I stood on the edge of the Grand Canyon I began to realize how huge nature is and how small and unimportant we are. You can't understand how deep the canyon is even when you see it. A huge argument in the car because all the motels were full and Dad had forgotten to call and reserve a room. We had to drive 80 miles to Flagstaff (Arizona) which is north of Phoenix. Mom and Dad argued all the way. Scott said if they didn't stop shouting at each other, he was going to get out and wait for a Greyhound bus. I need some new CDs. Tomorrow we cross the desert Death Valley through Nevada into California. I'm beginning to get worried. Will I like it there?

September 4: We've been in Livermore for a whole week now. However hard I try, I just don't like it here. It's so small and uninteresting. Street after street of houses with green lawns and cars outside. You can't get anywhere without a car. What will I do? Whenever I talk to Mom, she just tells me how beautiful it is here. And she expects me to think the same. She doesn't understand my problems! School starts the day after tomorrow. I'm nervous.

September 6: I HATE this place! I hate everything about this stupid place! It's terrible. School was a complete disaster. The kids laughed at me because of my Brooklyn accent. Just who do they think they are? And nothing seems to happen here. I mostly sit in my room and wish I was back home. Scott isn't too happy either. I heard him complain to a friend in Brooklyn on the phone.

September 9: Things are still bad at school, but I don't care if the other kids don't like me. They're all stupid anyway. Mom and Dad seem to like it here. So this place is OK for some people. Dad still hasn't bought me the pony he promised. I'll have to remind him again. At least he's not as tired and angry when he comes home in the evenings now. Scott has joined a basketball team. He practices all the time, so I've nobody to talk to anymore.

September 12: Wrote to Sally today and told her what a terrible place Livermore is and how unhappy I am. It was good to write it down.
A lot of people seem to go into San Francisco to work, so it's pretty dead here during the day. I rode around on my bike and went to the shopping center, but everything is so quiet. I'm too young to retire. What can I do? No concerts, no dances, nowhere to go. Can they make me stay here? I'll never forgive Mom and Dad for bringing me here.

September 17: Guess what! Our new neighbors came to see us today. They have a daughter my age called Cindy, and she's nice. We went to Pete's Pizza Place together, and I saw a boy from my English class – and he smiled at me. Maybe it won't be that bad here after all. At least there are some places to go – if you know where to find them.

September 18: I got my pony. He's called Skipper.
A neighbor lets me keep him in the field behind his house. I also met Mike (the guy who smiled at me yesterday) and we talked. We went to Pete's Pizza Place again and I met some of Mike's friends. I quite like them – and I even think they liked me! I've been invited to a party on the weekend.

September 23: Had my first date. Mike is real nice.
I think I might like it here after all.

(adaptiert aus: English G A4, Cornelsen, Berlin 1998, S. 107 – 108)

Aufgaben zu „Leaving home"

1. Maureen and Scott Donovan are moving to Livermore, California. Find out why.
  a) Markiere mit Textmarker im Text alle Stellen, die Auskunft zu dieser Frage geben.
  b) Kreuze dann das Zutreffende an.

Maureen and Scoot Donovan are moving to Livermore, California, because …

☐ … their relatives live there.
☐ … the weather there is better than in NYC.
☐ … their parents have found work there.
☐ … their parents want to go surfing.

2. When Maureen learns that she has to move to Livermore, she is shocked. Why doesn't she want to live there?
  a) Suche und markiere die Textstellen, aus denen hervorgeht, warum Maureen nicht nach Livermore ziehen möchte: ____________________
  b) Schreibe kurz auf, warum Maureen nicht nach Livermore ziehen möchte (natürlich auf Englisch!).

____

____

____

3. New York is very far away from California, but Maureen's parents decide to drive there instead of taking a plane. Why?
Markiere alle Stellen im Text, die Informationen zu dieser Frage geben. Kreuze dann alles Zutreffende an.

> **Tipp** *Lies noch einmal genau im Text nach, bevor du ankreuzt!*

Maureen's parents decide to drive to California because …

☐ **a)** … they want to check out the motels on the way.

☐ **b)** … they cannot afford the plane tickets.

☐ **c)** … they want their kids to get to know the US and to see the landscape.

☐ **d)** … Mrs Donovan is afraid of flying.

> **Zwischencheck: Wie bist du bisher vorgegangen?**
>
> In den Aufgaben 1 – 3 hast du geübt, wie man vorgehen kann, wenn man eine Information sucht, die im Text nicht direkt, sondern nur versteckt enthalten ist. Schaue dir die drei Aufgaben nochmals an und ergänze dann: Wenn ich eine Information suche, die im Text nicht direkt, sondern nur versteckt enthalten ist, dann gehe ich so vor:
>
> Ich beginne wie in Teil (a) der Aufgaben: Zuerst ______________________
>
> ____.
>
> Dann überlege ich anhand der markierten Stellen ______________________
>
> ____.

4. What does "out of this world" mean?
Als Maureen das Land der Indianer beschreibt, benutzt sie den Ausdruck „out of this world" (l. 52). Auch wenn du diesen Ausdruck nicht kennst, lässt sich aus dem Text erschließen, was „out of this world" hier auf Deutsch heißen könnte.

a) Schau noch einmal in den Zwischencheck, was du zuerst tun solltest.

b) Erläutere dann: „out of this world" könnte hier auf Deutsch bedeuten: ______________________

> **Tipp** *Denke auch bei den nächsten Aufgaben an den Zwischencheck: Überlege, was du vor der Beantwortung der Frage tun solltest!*

5. Why has the title "Leaving home" been chosen for this text?

a) Der Titel der Geschichte lautet „Leaving home". Warum wurde dieser Titel gewählt? Kreuze an und nenne eine Stelle, die deine Antwort belegt.

The title of the text is "Leaving home" because …

☐ … Maureen and Scott must listen to their father's geography lessons in the car.

☐ … Maureen and Scott move away from Brooklyn and leave their friends behind.

☐ … Maureen writes to Sally to tell her what a terrible place Livermore is.

☐ … Skipper can stay in the field behind Maureen's neighbor's house.

b) Gib eine Stelle an, die deine Antwort belegt: ______________________

READING

6. Right or wrong?

Entscheide aufgrund des Textes, ob folgende Aussagen zutreffen. Gib in der rechten Spalte eine Textstelle an, die deine Entscheidung belegt, und korrigiere unten die falschen Aussagen.

	right	wrong	line(s)
a) Mr Donovan has found a job in a law firm.	☐	☐	____
b) Maureen's friend in Brooklyn is called Cindy.	☐	☐	____
c) Scott has joined a baseball team in Livermore.	☐	☐	____
d) Mike is in Maureen's English class.	☐	☐	____

____

____

____

____

7. Mark the route the Donovans take on the map of the USA. Also mark the names of the states they drive through, the places they visit and add the events that seem important to you.

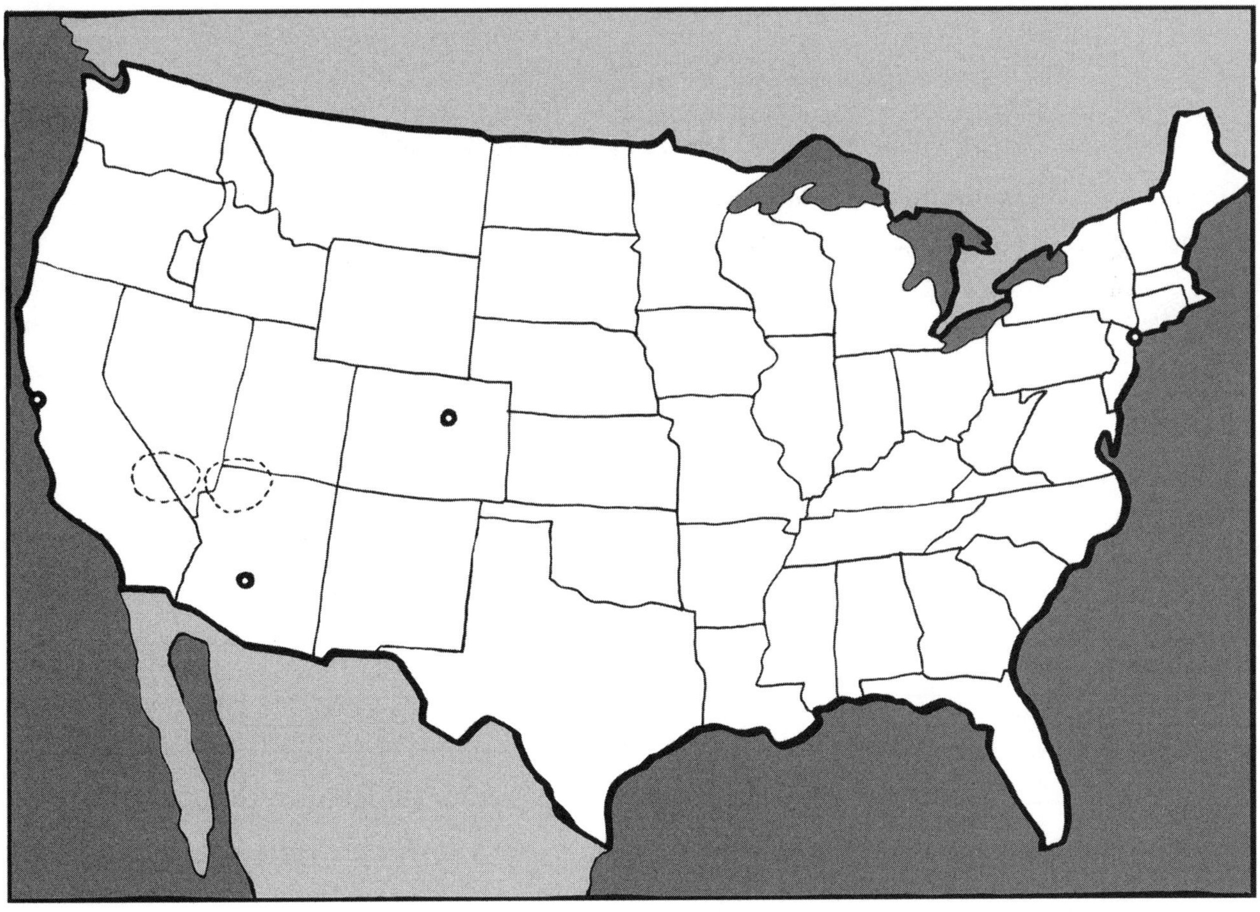

8. How does Maureen feel during the journey and her first days in Livermore – from her first diary entry on August 10 to her last one on September 23? There is a certain development.

a) Find out from the text why her feelings change. Draw a graph of Maureen's feelings. Mark the graph with numbers and write down the places and/or events and/or persons connected with it below the graph. Don't forget to give the lines from the text.

① *Lines 12 – 27: Maureen is shocked and sad (she is still in Brooklyn and has to say goodbye to her friends)*

② *Lines 28 – 42: bored (trip through Kansas with her family)*

③ ______________________________

④ ______________________________

⑤ ______________________________

⑥ ______________________________

⑦ ______________________________

⑧ ______________________________

⑨ ______________________________

b) Now divide the text into parts, according to Maureen's feelings. (You may find up to 9 parts!) Find a title for each one.

Part 1 goes from line ______________________ to ______________________.

Title: ____

Part 2 goes from line ______________________ to ______________________.

Title: ____

Part 3 goes from line ______________________ to ______________________.

Title: ____

Part 4 goes from line ______________________ to ______________________.

Title: ____

Part 5 goes from line ______________________ to ______________________.

Title: ____

Part 6 goes from line ______________________ to ______________________.

Title: ____

Part 7 goes from line ______________________ to ______________________.

Title: ____

Part 8 goes from line ______________________ to ______________________.

Title: ____

Part 9 goes from line ______________________ to ______________________.

Title: ____

An unknown nobody in the mountains

Informationen in Verbindung bringen

In Übungsbereich 3 übst du, verschiedene Informationen miteinander in Verbindung zu bringen und Schlussfolgerungen aus den Informationen zu ziehen.

Vorübungen

1. Schlussfolgerungen aus mehreren Sätzen ziehen

a) Hier sind drei Sätze abgedruckt, aus denen du eine Schlussfolgerung ziehen sollst:

Yellowstone is the oldest National Park. It was founded in 1872.
Yosemite National Park is located in the North East of California. It was founded in 1890.
Everglades National Park in Florida is famous for its alligators.

Welche der folgenden drei Schlussfolgerungen kann man aus den Sätzen ziehen?
(Lies alle Sätze genau und kreuze die richtige Lösung an.)

☐ Yellowstone is located in Florida.
☐ The second oldest National Park is Everglades National Park.
☐ No National Park in the United States was founded before 1872.

b) Hier sind wieder zwei Sätze abgedruckt. Nun sollst du selbst eine Schlussfolgerung ziehen:

In Yosemite you can watch bears, mountain lions and rattle snakes.
Grand Canyon National Park is famous for its condors, eagles and hawks.

Welche Schlussfolgerung kann man aus den zwei Sätzen ziehen? Formuliere einen Satz:

Bird watchers should ____.

2. Zusammengehörende Sätze finden

a) In drei der folgenden sechs Sätze geht es um dasselbe Thema. Welche drei Sätze sind das? Kreuze an.

☐ You go camping, fishing and hiking in Yellowstone.
☐ Yosemite Falls is the highest waterfall in the United States.
☐ You can go walking on over 800 miles of trails in High Country, Yosemite NP (National Park).
☐ Grand Canyon NP offers activities such as mule riding and wild water rafting.
☐ Maureen wants to spend her next vacation at the rim of the Grand Canyon.
☐ Mesa Verde NP was a former Indian settlement.

b) Welche Aussage passt zu diesen drei Sätzen?

☐ Different free time activities are offered in American National Parks.
☐ Maureen's father is a bird watcher.
☐ Yosemite NP is famous for its trees.

Übungen zu einem Text

Lies den folgenden Text in vier Schritten:

1. Vor dem Lesen: Überlege zunächst, was du schon über den Yosemite National Park und John Muir weißt.
2. Lesen ohne Bleistift: Überfliege zunächst einmal den Text, um zu sehen, worum es geht.
3. Lesen mit Bleistift für Randnotizen: Lies den Text nun gründlich mit einem Bleistift in der Hand. Unterstreiche wichtige Stellen und notiere am Rand in Stichworten, was du dort über den Yosemite National Park und John Muir erfährst.
4. Nach dem Lesen: Lies dir noch einmal deine Stichworte am Rand durch und überlege, was du nun über den Yosemite National Park und John Muir weißt.

Bearbeite dann die Aufgaben zum Text.

An unknown nobody in the mountains

A hundred years ago many people saw the United States as a huge country where they could use the land as they wanted. But one man realized before anybody else that nature was something we have to protect. That man was John Muir, the father of the National Parks.

In 1868, a tall young man got off a boat in San Francisco harbor. His name was John Muir. He had often traveled through the mountains, forests and canyons of the United States. It was his hobby to make notes about plants, wild animals and the geography of an area.
He was not a city man, and San Francisco with its population of 149,000 was not a place where he wanted to stay long. After five days he stopped somebody on the street and asked for "the nearest way out of town to the wild part of the state." "Where do you want to go?" the person asked. "Anywhere that's wild," was John Muir's answer. What he really meant was, in fact, Yosemite Valley. He had read a lot about it and now he wanted to visit it himself.

In those days Yosemite was already well-known to many Americans. In 1864, during the Civil War, President Lincoln had made the Yosemite Valley a state park so that farmers could not use it and settlers could not build homes or put up fences and walls. But in a country as big as the United States a law could soon be forgotten in an area so far away.

The journey to Yosemite was not easy. John Muir did not have enough money for a horse, so he and a friend had to walk for weeks through the Californian valleys, knee deep in flowers. When they entered Yosemite Valley for the first time, John Muir was fascinated by the views: the straight walls of El Capitan, the tree-covered floor of the valley, the silver line of water from Yosemite Falls. During the next years he went back again and again. "I love Yosemite like a mother loves a child," he once wrote. But as the years went by, his eyes saw something else: not only hotels and campsites, but also thousands of sheep; and he saw lots of workmen who were cutting down trees, even the famous Big Trees. On a visit in 1889, instead of open fields, he saw fences and cows. John Muir was horrified. But while he looked at the scene, his great idea was born – a system of National Parks where the land could be conserved and kept in its original state. As he wrote in a letter, "Everybody needs beauty as well as bread."
Over the years, John Muir became well-known as a conservationist. Through his work Yosemite National Park was established in 1890. Even the President of the United States wanted to meet him. In 1903 – 35 years after his first trip to Yosemite – John Muir and President Theodore Roosevelt camped alone in Mariposa Grove among the Big Trees, where they talked

together around a campfire. "I've had the best time of my life," said the president when he got back from their trip. As a result of those few days President Roosevelt decided that over a million acres of beautiful country-side should be made into National Parks. It was a great success for John Muir, but not the end of his long fight as a conservationist.

The fight for Hetch Hetchy

The city of San Francisco wanted to put a dam across Hetch Hetchy Valley. John Muir loved Hetch Hetchy. It was one of his favorite places in Yosemite National Park. This was what John Muir wrote in his diary: "It is sad that they want to dam Hetch Hetchy to supply San Francisco with water and electricity. They are going to flood it from wall to wall and bury its gardens two hundred feet deep. I can't sleep. This fight promises to be the worst ever."
John Muir realized that for all those people who were interested in conversation, there were so many who simply did not care. For Muir the battle for Hetch Hetchy became part of the universal battle between right and wrong. "That anybody should destroy this," he wrote, "is unbelievable. But sadly I have learned that there are people good enough and bad enough for anything."
On October 9th, 1909 – John Muir was now 71 years old – he had the chance to be alone with President Taft in a tour of Yosemite. Muir talked to him about conservation. The president listened carefully , but soon became tired. "But don't you think," said the president, "that we should use these valleys as they are so far from the centers of population?" And as a joke, the president pointed to the narrowest part of the canyon. "Now that would be a fine place for a dam." John Muir became very angry. "Dam Hetch Hetchy! Why not dam a cathedral or a church?"
The president became serious and listened more carefully. After their tour he stopped the project. But four years later, the United States had a new president, Woodrow Wilson, and the battle for Hetch Hetchy started again. John Muir wrote, "This is the 23rd year of my battle for Yosemite National Park." Then in December, "The battle for Hetch Hetchy is not yet lost. I still hope we will win."
Two days later, the US government gave the city of San Francisco permission to build the dam. Muir felt bitter. "I have done my best," he wrote. "It is a huge mistake ... a huge crime." But even then he hoped that people would see that the government was wrong; he hoped that people would get together and stop similar plans. But his dream did not come true. The dam was built. John Muir was tired, old, ill and alone. His wife and best friends, all had died before him. Friends and relatives tried to help him out of his loneliness and bitterness, but without success. He died on the morning of December 24th, 1914, one year after the decision to build the dam in Hetch Hetchy Valley.

(aus: English G B4. Cornelsen, Berlin 1998, S. 78–79, erzählt nach: Shirley Sargent: John Muir in Yosemite)

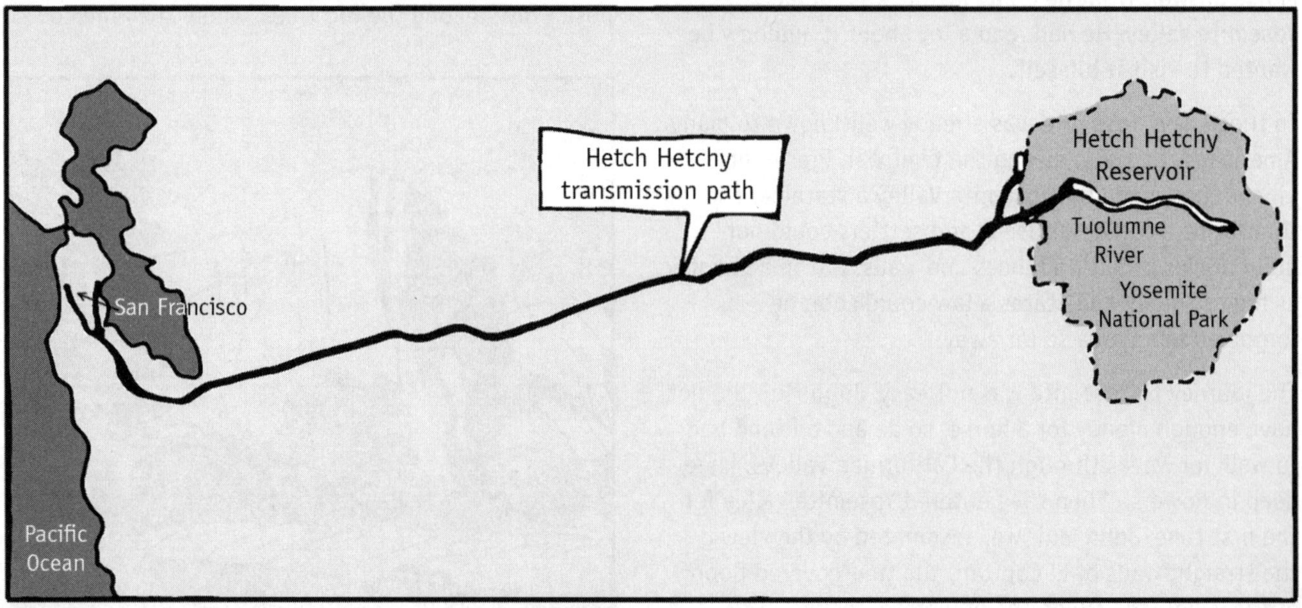

Aufgaben zu „An unknown nobody in the mountains"

1. After reading the text twice, draw a timeline of all important dates of Yosemite Valley and in the life of John Muir.

a) Im Text findest du Stellen markiert (unterstrichen), die dir helfen können, den Zeitstrahl zu erstellen. Ergänze:

In lines 78 – 81 we learn that on October 9th, 1909 John Muir ____________________

In lines 91 – 93 we learn that ____________________

b) Aus diesen Informationen kannst du schlussfolgern, in welchem Jahr der Kampf um Hetch Hetchy von neuem begann: ____________________

c) Unterstreiche nun alle anderen Stellen, die eine Zeitangabe und wichtige Informationen über das Yosemite Valley oder John Muirs Leben enthalten. Benutze wenn nötig unterschiedliche Farben.

d) Now start your time line. Enter the dates in chronological order. (Keep in mind that in a text the dates are sometimes not given chronologically.)

October 9th, 1909: John Muir talked to President Taft about the conservation of Hetch Hetchy.

Zwischencheck: Wie stelle ich Verbindungen zwischen Textstellen her?
In Aufgabe 1 hast du geübt, Verbindungen zwischen Textstellen herzustellen und daraus Schlüsse zu ziehen. Schaue dir die Aufgabe nochmals an und ergänze dann: Wenn ich Verbindungen zwischen verschiedenen Textstellen herstellen und daraus Schlüsse ziehen soll, dann gehe ich folgendermaßen vor:

Zuerst markiere ich ____

____.

Zur Unterscheidung benutze ich eventuell ______________________.

Dann verbinde ich ____

____.

Danach ____

____.

2. What did John Muir do for Yosemite Valley?
Bevor du die Frage beantwortest, sollst du entscheiden, ob die Aussagen unten über John Muir und den Yosemite National Park richtig oder falsch sind. Überlege dir zunächst Vorarbeiten, die dir nachher helfen können.

a) Vorarbeit: Markieren. Beschreibe, wie du vorgehst, und gehe entsprechend vor:

Zunächst unterstreiche ich alle Textstellen, die ______________________

____.

Anschließend verbinde ich zusammengehörende Stellen miteinander.

b) Kreuze nun an, ob die Aussagen zutreffen oder nicht. Gib in der rechten Spalte eine Stelle an, aus der man die Antwort erschließen kann.

	right	wrong	line(s)
1. Even before John Muir first went to Yosemite Valley, he was interested in nature.	☐	☐	____
2. Many Americans had lived in Yosemite Valley before Muir's first visit in 1868.	☐	☐	____
3. The idea of a system of National Parks came to John Muir when he saw the beauty of the valley.	☐	☐	____
4. Over the years Yosemite Valley changed, and John Muir did not like this.	☐	☐	____
5. Only a few people knew about John Muir's work as a conservationist.	☐	☐	____
6. President Roosevelt was interested in Muir's work and helped him.	☐	☐	____
7. During the fight for Hetch Hetchy, Muir realized that not many people were interested in conservation.	☐	☐	____
8. President Taft was interested in John Muir's work from the first moment on.	☐	☐	____
9. The fight for Hetch Hetchy ended after more than twenty years.	☐	☐	____
10. Muir was sad and disappointed about Woodrow Wilson's decision.	☐	☐	____

c) Now say in your own words what John Muir did for Yosemite Valley.

____

____

____

3. Find out why the city of San Francisco wanted to put a dam across Hetch Hetchy Valley.

Say which answers are right. (Don't forget to mark the important parts of the text!)

- ☐ **a)** They needed the water for the city of San Francisco.
- ☐ **b)** They wanted to use the reservoir for free time activities such as boat trips.
- ☐ **c)** They wanted to win electricity with the water from the reservoir.
- ☐ **d)** They wanted to build a cathedral there.

Which lines did you mark? ______________________________

4. Complete the sentences.

a) John Muir is called the father of National Parks because ______________________________

____

______________________________.

b) After his arrival in San Francisco in 1868 John Muir left the city after some days to ______________________________

____

______________________________.

c) John Muir died full of bitterness because ______________________________

____

______________________________.

READING

LERNFORTSCHRITTSERMITTLUNG

Name: ______________________ Class: __________ Date: ______________

Lies den folgenden Text mehrfach gründlich durch und beantworte dann die Fragen. Denke beim Lesen an die Schritte, die du in den Übungen angewandt hast!

The new girl

"Hey, look at the gook."

The word hit Lan harder than a hand, harder than a stick or a stone. Gook. Tears came to her eyes, but she tried to hide them, tried to smile politely and pretend that she had heard nothing. "And look at those clothes," said Wanda Potlowsky. "Where did she get them?"

Mother made them, Lan thought. During the quiet hours at night, after she has worked ten hours for low wages, in your wonderful country. That's where I got them. And she started to walk home, while the group of kids continued to laugh at her outside the school building.

Maureen was leaving school at the same time and she heard what the students had said. She recognized the new girl. Mrs Warburton had introduced her as a Vietnamese, or was it a Cambodian? Maureen couldn't remember. "Another immigrant," one of her friends had said. "How many more are going to come before the government finally decides that the country is full?" Maureen said nothing, although she had liked the girl when she had seen her in her class. Like many Asians she moved so beautifully and was so polite, always smiling. She had smiled then, although the others had been so cruel to her.

That evening Maureen said, "Mom, what does gook mean?"

"Where did you hear that expression?"

"We've got a new girl in class. One of the kids said it to her."

Mrs Donovan started to get angry. "It was very stupid to say something like that. Gook was a rude name that was used for the Vietcong during the Vietnam War. Is she Vietnamese?"

"I think so. We've got a lot of immigrants at the moment. Some of the kids say they're taking away our jobs and our places at college, and that the government ought to stop them. Is that true?"

"Who said that?" asked her father.

"Frank Minetti."

"Frank Minetti! What does he know? His parents were immigrants, too. And his father still can't speak English properly. Whenever I say something to him, he answers in Italian. What a lot of your friends forget is that we were all immigrants once. Now they talk as if they own the place. They should ask that Vietnamese girl why her family came here before they shut the door in her face."

Lan was very good at school. In art she was the best in class. It seemed obvious that in a few years she would win a price in a good college. Maureen wanted to talk to Lan, but a lot of the kids didn't like the Vietnamese, and Maureen didn't want to be the first who broke the ice. But then one day she went into the art room and found Wanda Potlowsky there. She was holding a picture that Lan had painted for a school competition.

"I hate this picture," said Wanda. "And Mrs Warburton says she's so good at art. How can she say that? It's terrible."

"What are you going to do with it?" asked Maureen.

"What am I going to do with it? Maybe I'm going to throw it out of the window."

"No," shouted Maureen. "You can't do that." She ran towards the girl to save the picture. The two girls fought until the picture fell on the floor. At once Wanda put her foot on it. The two girls stood opposite each other and their eyes met. Then Wanda turned around and left the room. Lan was standing at the door, but she said nothing as Wanda walked past her. Maureen picked up the picture. It showed a frightened family, the parents and three children – one of them a baby in the father's arms; they were running along a country road. The children were screaming. Behind them there were dark clouds of war. Wanda had stood on the faces of the children.

"I'm sorry," said Maureen. Lan took the picture. Her eyes were sad, but she smiled and said, "Thank you. It was very kind of you to try and save it. My father always said we must go to America. Everybody is free there, he often said. I never thought that people might not want us."

The two girls continued to talk and then Lan said, "Would you like to come to my house and meet my family?"

"Yes, please," said Maureen.

"I'll ask my parents tonight. Perhaps we can go after school tomorrow.

"The next day Maureen got off the bus with Lan and a group of other Vietnamese in a part of Brooklyn

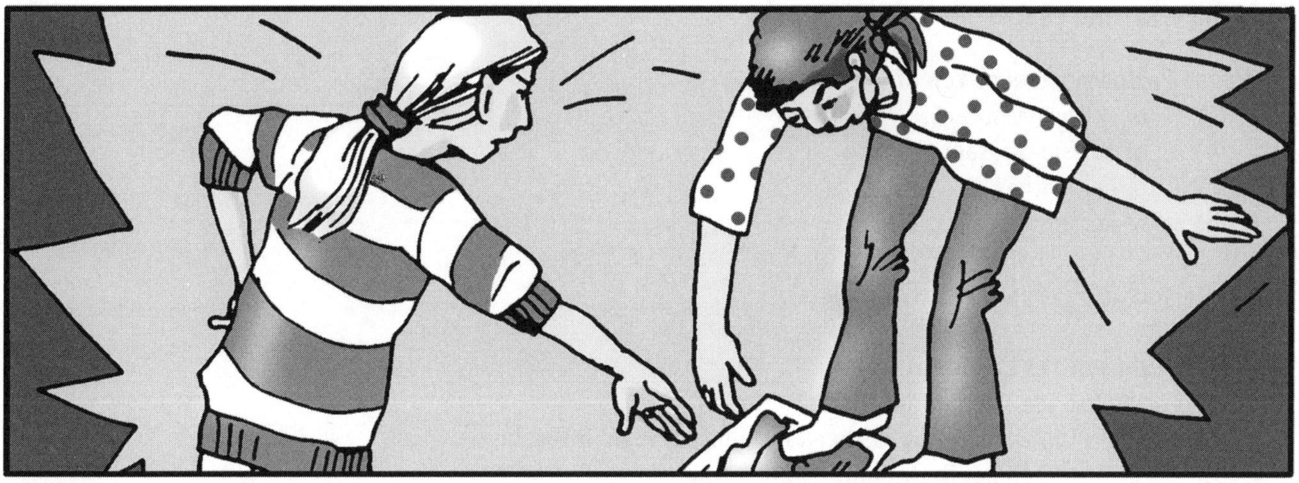

she didn't know very well. In the distance behind the large old buildings she heard a ship.
She supposed they must be near the harbor.
Maureen and Lan left the others and went alone down a long empty street.
A small boy walked next to them.
Maureen began to get nervous. "Don't worry," said Lan. "My brother will look after us."
Maureen looked down at the young boy. "This is a dangerous area. How can he look after us?"
"He is small, yes, but we are safe with him."
The boy looked up at Maureen and smiled confidently with his huge white teeth.
Lan's family lived on the fifth floor of a very old building. To get to the stairs you had to go down a long dark passage. The floor was covered with old boxes, newspapers and bottles; the smell was terrible. Suddenly Lan's brother stopped and listened. He said something quickly to his sister, and Lan pushed Maureen into a dark corner between a lot of old boxes. "Don't move," she said. They waited, and very soon a gang of kids ran past, followed a moment later by another gang. She heard shouts, glass broke, boxes fell over, and the whole time they stood still and never moved. Minutes passed and then Lan's brother went down the passage as quietly as a cat.
When he came back he said, "We can go now."
"What was that?" asked Maureen.
The boy smiled. "Dangerous place," he said.
Maureen was surprised how comfortable they had made their apartment with so few things.
"My father had a good business before we left Vietnam," said Lan. "My mother was a teacher.
At the moment Dad works in the harbor. Mom works in a food factory. I've told them what happened at school. They say we must work hard and be patient."
Lan's father offered Maureen a cup of tea.
"Nothing here is as bad as what we left behind."
Lan's mother had cooked a Vietnamese meal, and while they ate it Maureen heard how they had lived through years of war. They had spent all their money to buy places in a boat so that they could leave their country, but the captain had put too many families into a boat that was too small. They had spent weeks on the open sea; they had been attacked by pirates; they hadn't had enough food and water. Many died before they were finally found by a German boat. They had suffered all this to get to America. Just as her own Irish ancestors had probably suffered, Maureen thought.
"In your picture," she said, "there was a baby."
"My sister died on the journey," said Lan.
When it was time to go, Maureen thanked Lan and her parents for the meal. As it was already dark, she called her mother. Mrs Donovan shouted, "Where did you say you are? Don't try and walk! I'll be there in half an hour."
"My father will go down the street with you," said Lan, "so that you'll be safe."
Maureen thanked everybody again and left the apartment.
"You didn't say she lived here," said Mrs Donovan as they drove away towards their own neighborhood. Maureen looked out of the window at the kind, smiling man. "They're very nice people," she said. "That isn't an answer," said Mrs Donovan, but Maureen wasn't listening. She was thinking of her father's words: we were all immigrants once.

(aus: English G A4, Cornelsen, Berlin 1998, S. 31–32)

Working with the text

1. Wanda Potlowsky makes fun of Lan because ...

- ☐ **a)** ... of her heavy accent.
- ☐ **b)** ... of her big glasses.
- ☐ **c)** ... of her clothes.
- ☐ **d)** ... of her younger brother.

Where can you find this in the text? In line(s) ______________________________.

2. Maureen recognizes Lan because ...

- ☐ **a)** ... she has seen her before on the subway.
- ☐ **b)** ... she is in her class and has been introduced by their teacher.
- ☐ **c)** ... she has seen her in the youth group at her church.
- ☐ **d)** ... she is her brother's girlfriend.

Where can you find this in the text? In line(s) ______________________________.

3. Why does Lan wear homemade clothes?

____

____.

Where can you find this in the text? In line(s) ______________________________.

4. Which sentences are right and which are wrong? Also say where you can find this in the text.

	right	wrong	line(s)
a) Lan is a refugee from Cambodia.	☐	☐	____
b) Frank Minetti's father is an Italian immigrant.	☐	☐	____
c) Lan is very good at art.	☐	☐	____
d) Wanda Potlowsky likes Lan's drawing.	☐	☐	____

5. Here are some facts about Lan and the area where she lives. Which are right, which are wrong?
Again, say where you can find this in the text.

	right	wrong	line(s)
a) Lan and her family live in a quiet part of Queens.	☐	☐	____
b) Maureen knows this area very well.	☐	☐	____
c) Lan's family lives in an apartment on the first floor.	☐	☐	____
d) Their apartment is surprisingly comfortable.	☐	☐	____

6. What does "gook" mean in English?

____

____

____

7. How does Maureen know that Lan had a baby sister?

8. What was Lan's mother's job back in Vietnam?

9. What kind of work is Lan's mother doing in the United States?

READING

LÖSUNGEN ZU DEN ÜBUNGEN UND ZUR LERNFORTSCHRITTSERMITTLUNG

Übungsbereich 1	
Aufgabe	**Lösung**
Vorüb. 1	a) What, Ground Zero b) The place where the Towers stood is now called "Ground Zero". c) Ground Zero is the place where the Twin Towers of the World Trade Center stood.
Vorüb. 2	a) 19 hijackers b) (the Twin Towers of) the World Trade Center c) in the south of (the island of) Manhattan d) the "Tribute in Light"
Nr. 1	a) Sven Timmermann b) Zeile 3 c) a 19-year-old student (from Germany)
Nr. 2	a) When, arrive b) Zeilen 3 – 4 c) the night before
Zwischencheck	Zuerst markiere ich die wichtigen Wörter in der Frage. Ich suche und markiere im Text die Stellen, die zu den wichtigen Wörtern passen. Und schließlich beantworte ich die Frage.
Nr. 3	b) a jazz concert c) Washington Square, Lincoln Center, 42nd Street, 66th Street d) siehe U-Bahn-Plan auf S. 31
Nr. 4	b) Zeilen 35 – 44 c) he was frightened and nervous and therefore he took the wrong train
Nr. 5	a) the man who had taken the woman's bag b) The man was wearing the same leather jacket.
Nr. 6	a) wrong, lines 12 – 14 b) wrong, line 17 c) right, line 48 d) wrong, lines 48 – 49

Übungsbereich 2	
Aufgabe	**Lösung**
Vorüb. 1	mother, father; Irish
Vorüb. 2	b)
Vorüb. 3	a) Ireland; (very) poor and had nothing to eat b) meat
Nr. 1	b) their parents have found work there
Nr. 2	a) Zeilen 4 – 8 b) Maureen is used to living in a big city (Zeile 8). California is thousands of miles away (Zeile 10). Livermore is a small place (Zeile 10). Maureen is afraid she won't find such a good friend as Sally in Livermore (Zeilen 17 – 18). The guys at school say she will die of boredom there (Zeilen 18 – 19). Maureen likes Brooklyn (Zeile 27).
Nr. 3	c)
Zwischencheck	Zuerst suche und markiere ich alle Stellen, die zu der Frage passen. Dann überlege ich anhand der markierten Stellen, was die richtige Antwort ist.
Nr. 4	b) atemberaubend, toll (nicht von dieser Welt)
Nr. 5	a) Maureen and Scott move away from Brooklyn and leave their friends behind b) Zeilen 12 – 14
Nr. 6	a) wrong, lines 5 – 7 (Maureen's mother has found a job in a law firm, her father has found a job as a computer expert.) b) wrong, lines 16 and 115 (Maureen's friend in Brooklyn is called Sally. Cindy is the daughter of Maureen's

	neighbors in Livermore.) c) wrong, lines 100 – 101 (Scott has joined a basketball team.) d) right, line 116
Nr. 7	siehe Karte auf S. 31
Nr. 8	a) siehe Grafik auf S. 31 1. Lines 12 – 27: Maureen is shocked and sad (she is still in Brooklyn and has to say goodbye to her friends) 2. Lines 28 – 42: bored (trip through Kansas with her family) 3. Lines 43 – 50: things are getting more interesting in Colorado 4. Lines 51 – 75: amazed and impressed by nature (Indian land and the Grand Canyon) 5. Lines 75 – 85: a little nervous (a new city and a new school – on the way through Nevada to California) 6. Lines 86 – 112: angry, frustrated and lonely (after first day at school in Livermore) 7. Lines 113 – 119: things are starting to get better (new neighbors – Maureen goes to a pizza place with Cindy, the daughter of her new neighbors – she meets a boy from her English class, who smiles at her) 8. Lines 120 – 126: Maureen is reconciled (she's got her pony and has been invited to a party – she has a crush on Mike, the boy from her English class) 9. Lines 127 – 128: happy (after her first date with Mike) b) Abschnitte: siehe 8 a, Titel: individuelle Schülerlösungen

Übungsbereich 3	
Aufgabe	**Lösung**
Vorüb. 1	a) No National Park in the United States was founded before 1872. b) go to Grand Canyon National Park
Vorüb. 2	a) You go camping, fishing and hiking in Yellowstone. You can go walking on over 800 miles of trails in High Country, Yosemite NP. Grand Canyon NP offers activities such as mule riding and wild water rafting. b) Different free time activities are offered in American National Parks.
Nr. 1	a) … talked to President Taft about the conservation of Hetch Hetchy. … four years later, the United States had a new president, Woodrow Wilson, and the battle for Hetch Hetchy started again. b) 1913 d) 1864: President Lincoln made the Yosemite Valley a state park so that farmers could not use it and settlers could not build homes or put up fences or walls. 1868: John Muir visited Yosemite Valley for the first time. 1889: Muir discovered that farmers settled in Yosemite Valley and had put up fences. 1890: Yosemite National Park was established as a consequence of Muir's conservationist work. 1903: John Muir and President Theodore Roosevelt camped alone in Yosemite. October 9, 1909: John Muir talked to President Taft about the conservation of Hetch

Nr. 1	Hetchy Valley. The president stopped the project to build a dam through the valley. 1913: Under President Woodrow Wilson the battle for Hetch Hetchy started again, but Muir wrote he remained optimistic they could still win the battle. Two days later: The US government gave the city of San Francisco permission to build the dam. December 24, 1914: Muir died.
Zwischencheck	Zuerst markiere ich die wichtigen Stellen (nämlich diejenigen, in denen es um John Muir und Yosemite Valley geht). Zur Unterscheidung benutze ich eventuell unterschiedliche Farben. Dann verbinde ich Zusammengehörendes mit Pfeilen. Danach löse ich mithilfe dieser Informationen die Aufgabe.
Nr. 2	a) Zunächst unterstreiche ich alle Textstellen, die Informationen zu John Muir und Yosemite National Park enthalten. b) 1. right, lines 7 – 10 2. wrong, lines 23 – 24 3. wrong, lines 40 – 45 4. right, lines 36 – 40 5. wrong, lines 47 – 48 6. right, lines 49 – 58 7. wrong, there were many who were interested, but lots of them did not really care, lines 70 – 72 8. wrong, lines 80 – 86 9. right, lines 92 – 97 10. right, lines 97 – 98 c) John Muir tried to protect and preserve Yosemite Valley. He made it known to the greater public and succeeded in getting President Roosevelt interested in the valley. As a result, Roosevelt decided that Yosemite should be made a National Park.
Nr. 3	a) and c), lines 64 – 66
Nr. 4	a) he convinced President Roosevelt to turn over a million acres of beautiful countryside into National Parks b) explore the countryside of Yosemite Valley as he did not like life in the city c) he had not been able to prevent the dam across Hetch Hetchy Valley

Lernfortschrittsermittlung	
Aufgabe	**Lösung**
Nr. 1	c, lines 5 – 7
Nr. 2	b, lines 16 – 18 and 22
Nr. 3	Lan wears homemade clothes because her parents are poor. Her mother has to sew them at night (lines 8 – 11).
Nr. 4	a) wrong, lines 122 – 123 b) right, lines 41 – 45 c) right, lines 49 – 50 d) wrong, line 58
Nr. 5	a) wrong, lines 89 – 92 b) wrong, line 91 c) wrong, line 104 d) right, lines 120 – 121
Nr. 6	Gook was a rude name that was used for the Vietcong. [The Vietcong fought the USA and South Vietnamese governments during the Vietnam War (1959 – 75).]
Nr. 7	Lan had painted her family in the picture that Maureen tried to save from Wanda Potlowsky. The picture showed Lan's family running along a country road, fleeing from the war in their country, and it showed Lan's parents, her brother and a baby in her father's arms.
Nr. 8	She was a teacher.
Nr. 9	She works in a food factory (ten hours a day for low wages).

LÖSUNGEN ZU DEN ÜBUNGEN UND ZUR LERNFORTSCHRITTSERMITTLUNG

Zu Übungsbereich 1, Nr. 3 d

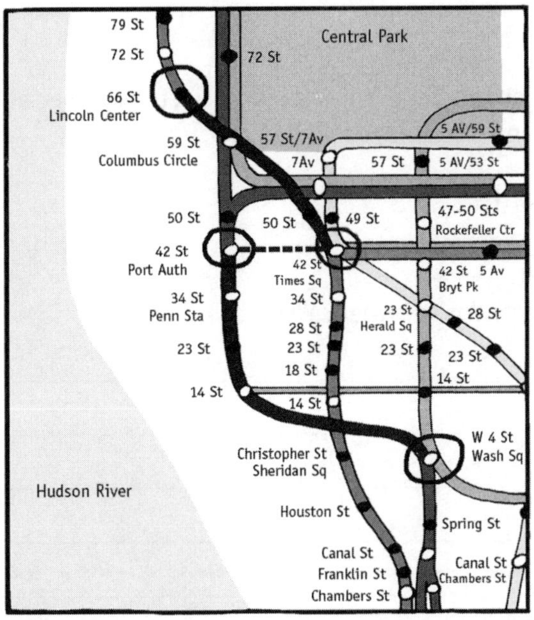

Zu Übungsbereich 2, Nr. 7

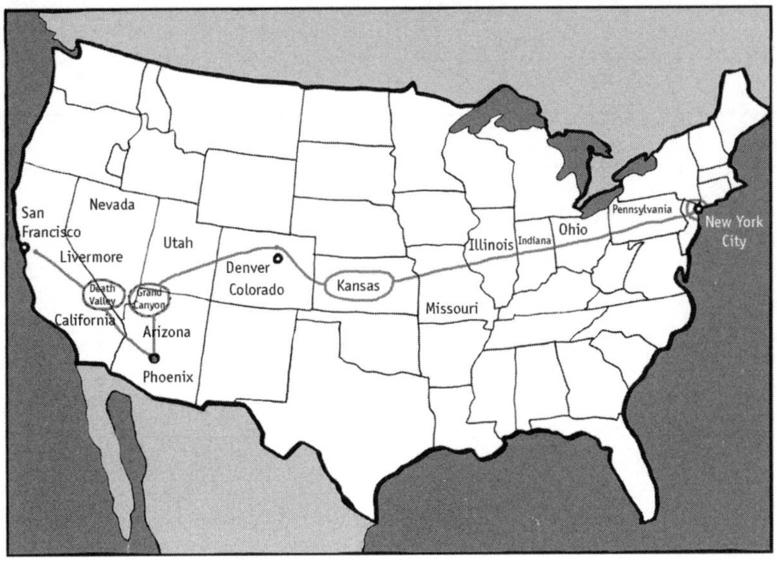

Zu Übungsbereich 2, Nr. 8 a

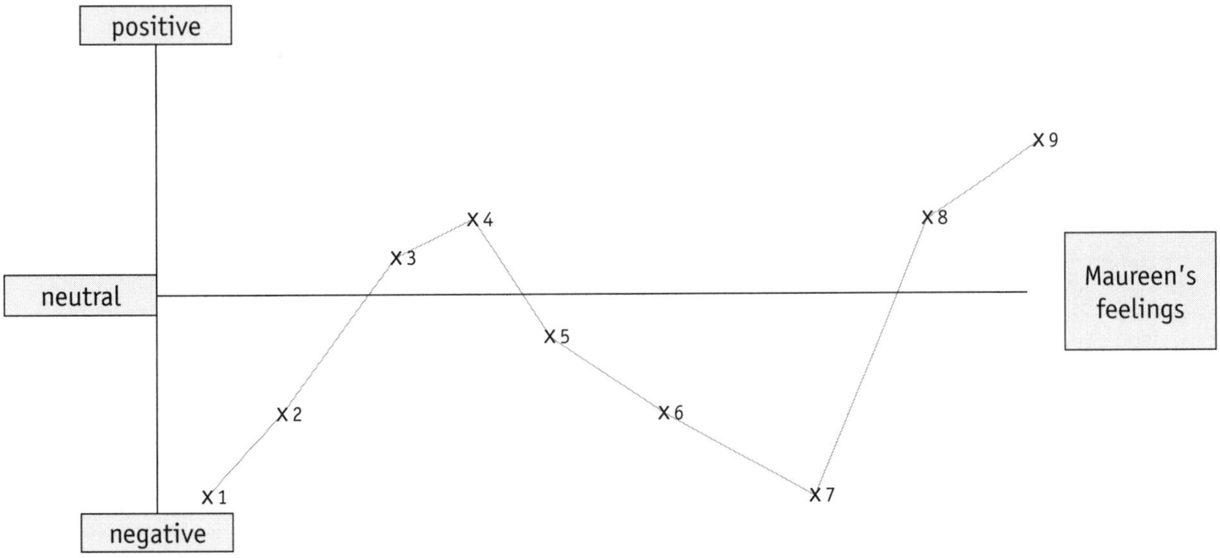

LERNSTANDSERMITTLUNG: REPORT

Name: ____________________ Class: __________ Date: __________

Write a report about a sport event or another event (e.g. an accident or a special day at your school). Write 120 – 150 words. Try to find an interesting headline first.

While writing the report do not forget:
- Give quick information on what happened.
- Give important information first.
- Answer the "five Ws" (Who? What? Where? When? Why?).

FEHLERANALYSE UND FÖRDEREMPFEHLUNGEN

	Kompetenzniveaustufe 1	**Kompetenzniveaustufe 2**	**Kompetenzniveaustufe 3**
Inhaltliche und formale Textgestaltung (Vollständigkeit, Richtigkeit, Eigenständigkeit, Adressatenorientierung und Textformat)	Der Text enthält zwar einzelne Aspekte des Ereignisses, aber es fehlen wesentliche Informationen, da nicht alle W-Fragen beantwortet werden. Der Bericht besteht aus nur wenigen Sätzen. Die Ereignisse sind zum größten Teil nicht chronologisch dargestellt, und der Einleitungssatz enthält nur wenige der wesentlichen Informationen. Der Hauptteil ist sehr knapp und gibt kaum Detailinformationen, die nicht von den wesentlichen Aspekten getrennt werden. Insgesamt ist der Text nicht durch Absätze strukturiert.	Der Text gibt einen grundlegenden Überblick über das Ereignis. Er beantwortet alle W-Fragen in Kürze. Die Ereignisse sind zum Teil chronologisch dargestellt, und der Einleitungssatz enthält einen großen Teil der wesentlichen Informationen. Im Hauptteil werden nur wenige Detailinformationen gegeben, die aber weitgehend von den wesentlichen Aspekten getrennt sind. Insgesamt ist der Text zumindest teilweise durch Absätze strukturiert.	Der Text gibt einen guten Überblick über das Ereignis. Er beantwortet alle W-Fragen. Die Ereignisse sind weitgehend chronologisch dargestellt, und der Einleitungssatz enthält (fast) alle wesentlichen Informationen. Im Hauptteil werden einige Detailinformationen gegeben, die meist von den wesentlichen Aspekten getrennt sind. Insgesamt ist der Text durch Absätze strukturiert.
Empfohlener Übungsbereich	Übungsbereich 1: Inhaltliche Textgestaltung	Übungsbereich 2: Inhaltliche Textgestaltung	Übungsbereich 3: Inhaltliche Textgestaltung
Sprachliche Textgestaltung (Wortschatz, Grammatik und Orthografie)	Der Schreiber/Die Schreiberin verfügt über einen sehr eingeschränkten Grundwortschatz, es kommen häufig elementare Fehler und Wortwiederholungen vor. *Linking words* werden nicht/kaum verwendet. Der Schreiber/Die Schreiberin verwendet zwar nicht immer vollständige Sätze, dennoch ist der Text auch für einen *Native Speaker* im Großen und Ganzen verständlich. Bei der Verwendung des *simple past* und Adjektiv/Adverb bestehen noch große Unsicherheiten in der Bildung und Anwendung. Auch bei der Einhaltung der *word order* zeigen sich noch beträchtliche Schwierigkeiten. Insgesamt kommen noch häufig elementare Grammatikfehler vor. Der Schreiber/Die Schreiberin beachtet kaum die Regeln der Orthografie.	Der Schreiber/Die Schreiberin kann den Grundwortschatz zumindest grundlegend anwenden, es kommen aber noch elementare Fehler und Wortwiederholungen vor. *Linking words* werden zum Teil verwendet. Der Schreiber/Die Schreiberin verwendet weitgehend vollständige Sätze, die auch für einen *Native Speaker* weitgehend verständlich sind. Bei der Verwendung des *simple past* und Adjektiv/Adverb kommen noch Fehler bei der Bildung und/oder Anwendung vor. Auch die *word order* ist zum Teil noch fehlerhaft. Insgesamt kommen noch elementare Grammatikfehler vor. Der Schreiber/Die Schreiberin verstößt noch häufig gegen die Regeln der Orthografie.	Der Schreiber/Die Schreiberin kann den Grundwortschatz weitgehend sicher und abwechslungsreich anwenden, es kommen aber noch gelegentlich Fehler und Wortwiederholungen vor. *Linking words* werden häufiger verwendet. Der Schreiber/Die Schreiberin verwendet fast durchgehend vollständige Sätze, die auch für einen *Native Speaker* verständlich sind. Bei der Verwendung des *simple past* und Adjektiv/Adverb kommen nur noch gelegentlich Fehler bei der Bildung und/oder Anwendung vor. Auch im Bereich *word order* zeigen sich noch kleinere Schwierigkeiten. Insgesamt kommen noch gelegentlich elementare Grammatikfehler vor. Der Schreiber/Die Schreiberin verstößt gelegentlich gegen die Regeln der Orthografie.
Empfohlener Übungsbereich	Übungsbereich 1: Sprachliche Textgestaltung	Übungsbereich 2: Sprachliche Textgestaltung	Übungsbereich 3: Sprachliche Textgestaltung

Teil 1: Inhaltliche Textgestaltung

Writing a report about a handball match

Steffen is writing a report about a match of his school's U14 team. It is for the English page of his school magazine. Read it and find out how you can make it better (and shorter). Which information is important? Which information is not so important?

> **Tipp** *Unterstreiche die wichtigen Sätze grün, die unwichtigen rot.*

Handball: Vesalius beaten by Leni Valk

Leni Valk School beat Andreas Vesalius School 27 : 22 in Keppenberg last Wednesday. It was the first sunny and hot day of the year, so the air was a little bit sticky in the gym. It was the schools' cup semi-final.
The match started 20 minutes late because Leni Valk's coach driver could not find the gym in Keppenberg. Andreas Vesalius had a better start and soon the score was 7 : 2 for their team. Lars Lettgen scored the first four goals for his team. After 15 minutes Leni Valk got better and their best player Steffen Wagner scored six goals in the first half. At halftime the score was 12 : 11 for Andreas Vesalius. The spectators went outside in the break and enjoyed the sun.
The second half was even more exciting. Leni Valk's goalkeeper Dominik Koller, who was wearing a pink jersey, became the best player of his team. He managed to catch some of the most difficult throws of Andreas Vesalius's players. Andreas Vesalius's players were disappointed and made many mistakes. One of their players changed his shoes, but this did not help. The final score was 27 : 22 for Leni Valk. They will play the final in Wildenbach next week. Their coach was happy and she bought them an ice-cream on their way back.

It will be easier for you to make the report better, if you find the information that answers the "W"-questions. Make notes.

Who? ______________________ What? ______________________

Where? ______________________ Why? ______________________

When? ______________________ How? ______________________

Now write the final report:

____

____

____

____

____

____

Das solltest du beim Schreiben eines Berichts über ein Spiel oder ein Ereignis beachten:
- Teile deinem Leser schnell erkennbar mit, was passiert ist.
- Beginne zunächst mit den wichtigen Informationen.
- Gib danach Detailinformationen.

Achte darauf, dass du immer Informationen über die „5 Ws" (**Who? What? Where? When? Why?** und manchmal auch **How?**) gibst.

Teil 2: Sprachliche Textgestaltung

Working with words

Hier übst du Wörter, die wichtig sind, wenn du einen Bericht über einen Unfall oder ein Sportereignis schreiben möchtest.

Accident and sports words

Read the descriptions and match them with the right word.

1. When two cars crash.
2. In a handball match each team tries to hit the ... of the other team.
3. Someone who plays in a match.
4. Someone who drives a car or a bus.
5. A car that takes you to hospital after an accident.
6. In a football match each ... lasts 45 minutes.
7. When you are badly injured they take you to ... after an accident.
8. He fell down and ... his knee.
9. When two teams play against each other.
10. When one car drives into another.
11. At the end of the match the ... was 4 : 3.
12. They have got red, yellow and green lights and tell you, when you must stop and when you can go.

- ☐ crash
- ☐ ambulance
- ☐ hospital
- ☐ halftime
- ☐ accident
- ☐ driver
- ☐ traffic lights
- ☐ player
- ☐ score
- ☐ match
- ☐ goal
- ☐ hurt

Now mark all the accident words yellow and all the sports words blue.
Be careful: There is one word, which is both an accident and a sports word.

Working with grammar

Hier übst du die Bildung und die Verwendung des *simple past* in bejahten und verneinten Sätzen. Lies dir zunächst die Regeln in dem Kasten durch und bearbeite dann die Aufgabe auf der nächsten Seite.

Du bildest das *simple past,* indem du bei **regelmäßigen Verben** -ed anhängst: *laugh + -ed = laughed.*
Beachte folgende Besonderheiten bei der Schreibweise:
- Ein -y wird nach einem Konsonanten zu -i: *try – tried*
- Ein stummes -e entfällt: *love – loved*
- Einige Konsonanten werden verdoppelt: *plan – planned*

Bei den **unregelmäßigen Verben** verwendest du die 2. Form, z. B. *see – saw.* Diese Formen musst du auswendig lernen:
Beachte: *was* ist die Vergangenheit von *is/am, were* von *are.*
Eine Aussage im *simple past* verneinst du mit *didn't (did not)* + Infinitiv (Grundform des Verbs).
Beachte: Die Verneinung von *was* ist *wasn't (was not),* die von *were* ist *weren't (were not).*

Mit dem *simple past* kannst du über Vergangenes berichten, z. B. wenn du einen Bericht über einen Unfall oder ein Sportereignis schreibst. Häufig verwendet man Zeitangaben wie *yesterday, last week* oder *some months ago.*

WRITING

Simple past: An accident

Put the infinitives into the simple past.

> **Tipp** *Die unterstrichenen Verben sind unregelmäßig. Schlage sie nach, falls du dir unsicher bist.*

Yesterday there __________________ *(be)* a bad accident in Dinslaken. A 14 year-old boy __________________ *(be)* on his way home from school. He __________________ *(ride)* his bike along Goethe Street and __________________ *(try)* to cross Voerder Street. A 44 year-old teacher, who __________________ *(be)* also on his way home, __________________ *(not see)* the bike and __________________ *(crash)* into the boy. The boy __________________ *(fly)* over the teacher's car and __________________ *(land)* on the cycle track. The teacher __________________ *(stop)* his car and __________________ *(run)* to the boy, who was lying on the ground. The boy ____________________________________ *(cannot speak)* and __________________ __________________ *(cannot move)* because he __________________ *(be)* unconscious. Another pupil, who had seen the accident, __________________ *(call)* the police and an ambulance with his mobile. When the ambulance __________________ *(arrive)*, they __________________ *(take)* the 14-year-old boy to hospital. The teacher's car __________________ *(not be)* seriously damaged, so he ______________________________ *(can drive)* home.

Working with sentences

Hier übst du die Wortstellung bei Orts- und Zeitangaben.

> Zeitangaben können am Anfang oder am Ende eines Satzes stehen. Ortsangaben stehen meist am Ende. Stehen beide Angaben am Ende, so nennst du zuerst die Ortsangabe und dann die Zeitangabe.

Place and time

Find the right place for the words in brackets and write down the complete sentences.

a) (in Brichthausen) – Yesterday there was a football match between Brichthausen SV and SV Union Repoberg.

____

b) (at 2 p.m.) – The match started.

____

c) (in the tenth minute) – The first goal was shot.

____

d) (in the break, into the changing room) – It started to rain and both teams went.

____

e) (next week, in Brichthausen) – The two teams will finish the game.

____

Teil 1: Inhaltliche Textgestaltung

Writing a report about an accident

Sarah has seen an accident and wants to write a report for her school magazine. Now she is studying her notes. Some of them are important, others aren't. All the facts are not in the correct order. Can you help her to arrange the important facts in the correct order?

> **Tipp**
> *Unterstreiche die wichtigen und unwichtigen Sätze mit zwei verschiedenen Farben.*
> *Bringe die wichtigen Sätze dann in die richtige Reihenfolge.*

☐ teacher had a broken leg – ambulance took him to hospital
☐ two injured – car accident
☐ yesterday – a bad car accident in Dinslaken
☐ two people injured
☐ a 19 year-old driver from Voerde – cross Park Road
☐ a yellow T-shirt – blue jeans
☐ she – not hurt – her younger brother – hospital
☐ never – hospital before
☐ I – only reporter – there
☐ able to leave – hospital – evening
☐ luckily – not badly hurt
☐ she – didn't see the car of a 52 year-old teacher from Wesel who was driving along Garden Street
☐ he – a nice blue car – wanted to drive to a friend
☐ teacher and paramedic – good friends
☐ two cars crashed into each other – stopped against a tree
☐ road – closed for the general traffic – two hours
☐ both cars – damaged
☐ both drivers – buy a new safe car – as soon as possible
☐ warm and sunny day – birds were flying up in the sky
☐ police and ambulance – came after only five minutes

Now write the complete report and make paragraphs for new ideas. Use linking words where possible.

Two injured in car accident

Teil 2: Sprachliche Textgestaltung

Working with words

Hier übst du Wörter, die wichtig sind, wenn du einen Bericht über einen Unfall oder ein Sportereignis schreiben möchtest.

Accident and sports words

Do the crossword puzzle.

Across:

1. When someone in a team doesn't play well, they ... him and he must sit down, while another player goes into the match.
2. In a football match each ... lasts 45 minutes.
3. The old lady wanted to ... Willow Road when she crashed into a bike.
4. Yesterday two people were badly ... in a car accident.
5. The boy was walking ... Bury-St.-Edmund-Street, when a car hit him.

Down:

6. There were many cars, busses and lorries in town today, so there was a lot of ...
7. There were 32 teams in the Fifa World Cup 2006, but only two teams (Italy and France) were in the ...
8. Someone who works in an ambulance.
9. Their best player ... *(simple past)* five goals.
10. Someone who tells the players how to train and what to do in a match.

Now mark all the accident words yellow and all the sports words blue.

Working with grammar

Hier übst du die Bildung und die Verwendung des *simple past.* Lies dir zunächst die Regeln in dem Kasten durch und bearbeite dann die Aufgabe.

Du bildest das *simple past,* indem du bei **regelmäßigen Verben** -ed anhängst: *laugh + -ed = laughed.*
Beachte folgende Besonderheiten bei der Schreibweise:
- Ein -y wird nach einem Konsonanten zu -i: *try – tried*
- Ein stummes -e entfällt: *love – loved*
- Einige Konsonanten werden verdoppelt: *plan – planned*

Bei den **unregelmäßigen Verben** verwendest du die 2. Form, z. B. *see – saw.* Diese Formen musst du auswendig lernen:
Beachte: *was* ist die Vergangenheit von *is/am, were* von *are.*

Eine Aussage im *simple past* verneinst du mit *didn't (did not)* + Infinitiv (Grundform des Verbs).
Beachte: Die Verneinung von *was* ist *wasn't (was not),* die von *were* ist *weren't (were not).*

Mit dem *simple past* kannst du über Vergangenes berichten, z. B. wenn du einen Bericht über einen Unfall oder ein Sportereignis schreibst. Häufig verwendet man Zeitangaben wie *yesterday, last week oder some months ago.*

Simple past: A wet football match

Fill in the right verb from the box. Don't forget to use the simple past.

Tipp *Überlege dir zuerst, ob die Verben regelmäßig oder unregelmäßig sind.*

be (2x) – be able to – become – cannot play – cannot see – end – fall down – get (2x) – have (2x) – hurt – not have – play – score – start (2x) – stop

Rain stopped football match

Yesterday Brichthausen SV __________ against SV Union Repoberg in Brichthausen. The match __________ at 3 p.m. and Brichthausen __________ the first goal in the tenth minute. Then the match __________ a bit slow because both teams __________ some difficulties. Brichthausen __________ a new goalkeeper because their regular one __________, he had broken his hand. Repoberg's team __________ quite new and __________ much time to train. Just before halftime Ferdinand Müller __________ score a hit, so the first half __________ 1 : 1. In the break it __________ to rain and it __________ worse in the second half. Soon it was pouring down and the players __________ anything because the rain __________ so heavy. The grass on the football pitch __________ very slippery and when the first players __________ and __________ themselves, the trainers __________ the match. It will be finished next week in Repoberg.

Working with sentences

Hier übst du die Wortstellung bei Orts- und Zeitangaben.

Zeitangaben können am Anfang oder am Ende eines Satzes stehen. Ortsangaben stehen meist am Ende. Stehen beide Angaben am Ende, so nennst du zuerst die Ortsangabe und dann die Zeitangabe.

Place and time

Find the right place for the words in brackets and write down the complete sentences.

a) (in Dinslaken, yesterday) – A bad accident happened.

b) (after school, along Goethe street) – A 14-year old boy was cycling when a teacher crashed into him.

c) (in only seconds, over the teacher's car, on the ground) – The boy flew and landed.

d) (from the bus stop) – One of his classmates saw the accident and called the ambulance, which came very soon.

e) (into the ambulance) – The paramedics put the injured boy.

f) (after five minutes, at the hospital) – The ambulance arrived.

Zum Schluss wird es noch einmal schwerer: Hier ist der Satz vollständig durcheinandergeraten, und du musst nicht nur die Orts- und Zeitangaben an die richtige Stelle setzen, sondern auch Subjekt, Prädikat und Objekt sortieren.

g) in hospital – examined – a doctor – the boy – ten minutes later

Teil 1: Inhaltliche Textgestaltung

Writing a report

You have just watched an exciting match or another event. Now you want to write a report about it for the English page of your school magazine. Write the report in your exercise book.

Tipp *Beachte beim Schreiben deines Berichts die Hinweise in dem Kasten und hake die erledigten Punkte ab.*

Tips for writing a good report

Always follow these three steps: pre-, while- and post-writing.

1. Pre-writing

- ☐ Collect ideas and organize them (use one of the following three methods).
- – Answer the 5 Ws and make notes: Who? Where? When? What? Why?

____

____

____

- – Use a mind map.

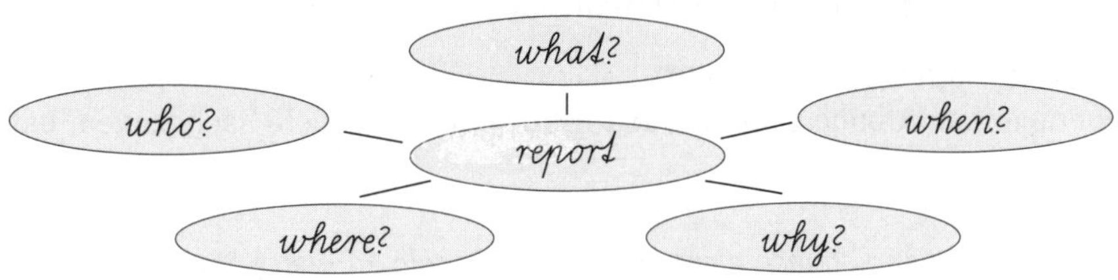

- – Arrange the information in a chart.

Where?	When?	What?	Why?

2. While-writing

- ☐ Tell the reader at the beginning what the report is about.
- ☐ Give the most important information first.
- ☐ Then give necessary details.
- ☐ Make paragraphs for new ideas (e.g. first half, second half).
- ☐ Make sure that you include the 5 Ws.

3. Post-writing

Before you send the report to the editor of your school magazine, you should read it several times and answer the following questions:

- ☐ Is the report complete? Are there answers to all 5 Ws?
- ☐ Does the reader get a quick information about the main facts?
- ☐ Does the report have unimportant information? If so, delete it.
- ☐ Check your report carefully for mistakes.

Tipp *Make a personal checklist with your most common mistakes and use it for revising your reports.*

Teil 2: Sprachliche Textgestaltung

Working with words

Hier wiederholst du Wörter, die wichtig sind, wenn du einen Bericht über einen Unfall oder ein Sportereignis schreibst.

Accident and sports words

Make a mind map for accident words and one for sports words.

> **Tipp** *Finde zuerst Oberbegriffe wie* people, activities/verbs, places *usw. und trage dann zu jedem Begriff möglichst viele Wörter ein.*

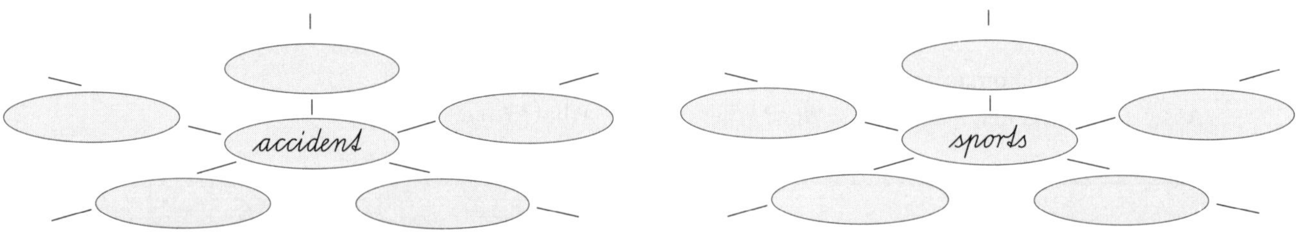

Working with grammar

Hier übst du die Bildung und die Verwendung des *simple past.*

Using the simple past in a report

Bevor du mit der Übung beginnst, solltest du über die Regeln nachdenken, indem du den Kasten vervollständigst.

> **Tipp** *Wenn du dich nicht mehr an die Regeln erinnerst, schaue auf Seite 39 nach.*

Die Bildung des *simple past:*

- Regelmäßige Verben: ______________________________
- Unregelmäßige Verben: ______________________________

Die Verwendung des *simple past:*

Man verwendet das *simple past,* wenn man über ______________________ schreiben möchte.

Hier kannst du die Signalwörter zum *simple past* aufschreiben: ______________________________

____

Now read the report you have written in "Inhaltliche Textgestaltung" once again. (If you haven't written it, please do so now.)
Then check your verbs and tick off the things you have done:

- ☐ Underline all the verbs in the text.
- ☐ Check if they are really in the simple past.
- ☐ Did you use the second form for the irregular verbs? Your English book can help you.
- ☐ Did you use the correct form of the regular verbs?
- ☐ Correct your mistakes.

> **Tipp** *Verben sind Tätigkeitswörter und beschreiben, was jemand macht.*
> *Du solltest in jedem Satz mindestens ein Verb haben.*

Working with sentences

Hier übst du die Wortstellung bei Orts- und Zeitangaben.

Place and time

Bevor du die Aufgabe erledigst, solltest du über die Regeln nachdenken, indem du die Lücken in dem Kasten füllst.

Englische Sätze sind fast immer nach dem gleichen Muster aufgebaut: Subjekt – Prädikat – Objekt. Zeitangaben stehen meist ____________________ oder ____________________ des Satzes. Ortsangaben stehen ____________________ des Satzes. Enthält ein Satz sowohl eine Orts- als auch eine Zeitangabe, so steht zuerst die ____________________, dann die ____________________.

Now use the following notes to form sentences. Be careful with the word order.

a) in Duisburg – an accident – yesterday – happened – in front of a school

____

b) two pupils – onto the street – ran – after school – without watching for traffic

____

c) at the bus stop – at the same time – in front of the school – arrived – the bus

____

d) the boys – saw – on the street – the bus driver

____

e) couldn't stop – he – the bus – in time – but

____

f) the bus – the two pupils – hit

____

g) on the pavement* – flew – and landed – through the air – they

____

h) arrived – the ambulance – soon – at the school – to hospital – the two boys – and took

____

____

*pavement: Bürgersteig

Übungsbereich 1

Writing a report about a handball match

Handball: Vesalius beaten by Leni Valk

Leni Valk School beat Andreas Vesalius School 27 : 22 in Keppenberg last Wednesday. It was the schools' cup semi-final.

Andreas Vesalius had a better start and soon the score was 7 : 2 for their team. Lars Lettgen scored the first four goals for his team. After 15 minutes Leni Valk got better and their best player Steffen Wagner scored six goals in the first half. At halftime the score was 12 : 11 for Andreas Vesalius.

The second half was even more exciting. Leni Valk's goalkeeper Dominik Koller became the best player of his team. He managed to catch some of the most difficult throws of Andreas Vesalius's players. Andreas Vesalius's players were disappointed and made many mistakes.

The final score was 27 : 22 for Leni Valk. They will play the final in Wildenbach next week.

Working with words

1. When two cars crash: accident.
2. In a handball match each team tries to hit the goal of the other team.
3. Someone who plays in a match: player.
4. Someone who drives a car or a bus: driver.
5. A car that takes you to hospital after an accident: ambulance.
6. In a football match each halftime lasts 45 minutes.
7. When you are badly injured they take you to hospital after an accident.
8. He fell down and hurt his knee.
9. When two teams play against each other: match.
10. When one car drives into another: crash.
11. At the end of the match the score was 4 : 3.
12. They have got red, yellow and green lights and tell you, when you must stop and when you can go: traffic lights.

Accident words: accident, driver, ambulance, hospital, crash, traffic lights

Sports words: goal, player, halftime, match, score

Accident and sports word: hurt

Working with grammar

was, was, rode, tried, was, didn't see, crashed, flew, landed, stopped, ran, couldn't speak, couldn't move, was, called, arrived, took, wasn't, could drive

Working with sentences

a) Yesterday there was a football match between Brichthausen SV and SV Union Repoberg in Brichthausen.

b) The match started at 2 pm./At 2 pm the match started.

c) In the tenth minute the first goal was shot./ The first goal was shot in the tenth minute.

d) In the break it started to rain and both teams went into the changing room./It started to rain in the break and …

f) The two teams will finish the game in Brichthausen next week.

Übungsbereich 2

Writing a report about an accident

Two injured in car accident

Yesterday there was a bad car accident in Dinslaken. Two cars crashed into each other and stopped against a tree. Two people were injured.

A 19 year-old driver from Voerde wanted to cross Park Road. She did not see the car of a 52 year-old teacher from Wesel who was driving along Garden Street. She was not hurt, but her younger brother was taken to hospital. Luckily he was not badly hurt, so he was able to leave the hospital in the evening. The teacher had a broken leg and the ambulance took him to hospital.

The police and ambulance came after only five minutes and the road was closed for the general traffic for two hours. Both cars were totally damaged.

Working with words

Accident words: cross, injured, along, traffic, paramedic
Sports words: replace, halftime, final, scored, coach, (injured)

Working with grammar
played, started, scored, got/became, had, had, couldn't play, was, didn't have, was able to, ended, started, got/became, couldn't see, was, became/got, fell down, hurt, stopped

Working with sentences

a) A bad accident happened in Dinslaken yesterday./ Yesterday a bad accident happened in Dinslaken.

b) A 14-year old boy was cycling along Goethe street after school when a teacher crashed into him./After school a 14-year old boy was cycling along Goethe street when a teacher crashed into him.

c) In only seconds the boy flew over the teacher's car and landed on the ground.

d) One of his classmates saw the accident from the bus stop and called the ambulance, which came very soon.

e) The paramedics put the injured boy into the ambulance.

f) The ambulance arrived at the hospital after five minutes.

g) Ten minutes later a doctor examined the boy in hospital.

Übungsbereich 3

Writing a report
Individuelle Lösungen

Working with words
Individuelle Lösungen, zum Beispiel:
Accident: people: driver, man, woman, boy, girl, paramedic, policeman/policewoman, places: on the road, to hospital, on the ground, cycle track, activities: to crash, to walk/drive along, to cross a road, to turn left/right, to fall down, to ride his/her bike, to stop, to call an ambulance, to take to hospital, things: traffic, traffic jam, traffic lights, ambulance, after the accident: not hurt, injured, broken arm/leg, unconscious
Sports: people: player, goalkeeper, referee, coach, supporter, dancer, places: stadium, gym, field, football pitch, tennis court, swimming pool, running track, ski slope, activities: to score a goal, to run, to jump, to hit the goal, to ride, to swim, to dance, to train, to shoot, to win, to lose, to beat, things: goal, score, football, tennis racket, table tennis bat, skis, saddle, bike, helmet, running shoes, final, semi-final, championship, cup, halftime, shot, medal

Working with grammar
Regelmäßige Verben: Verb + ed, unregelmäßige Verben: 2. Form
Man verwendet das *simple past,* wenn man über Vergangenes, z. B. Unfälle oder Sportereignisse, berichten möchte.
Signalwörter: yesterday, last week/month/..., a week/month/some time/... ago, in 2008

Working with sentences
Zeitangaben stehen meist am Anfang oder am Ende des Satzes. Ortsangaben stehen am Ende des Satzes. Enthält ein Satz sowohl eine Orts- als auch eine Zeitangabe, so steht zuerst die Ortsangabe, dann die Zeitangabe.

a) Yesterday an accident happened in front of a school in Duisburg.

b) After school two pupils ran onto the street without watching for traffic.

c) At the same time the bus arrived at the bus stop in front of the school.

d) The bus driver saw the boys on the street.

e) But he couldn't stop the bus in time.

f) The bus hit the two pupils.

g) They flew through the air and landed on the pavement.

h) Soon the ambulance arrived at the school and took the two boys to hospital.

Name: ______________________ Class: __________ Date: ______________

Write a report about a sport event or another interesting event. Find a suitable headline for your report and tell your reader what happened. Don't forget to give all the important information.

Name: ____________________ Class: __________ Date: __________

Write a biography about a famous person (an actress/actor, a singer, a sportswoman/-man, a writer, a politician, a scientist).

First collect information about the person (for example in a library or on the Internet). Then write a biography of 120 – 150 words.

You should write about:
- when and where the famous person was born
- his or her family
- how his or her career began
- why people know him or her
- what his or her first great success was
- …

	Kompetenzniveaustufe 1	**Kompetenzniveaustufe 2**	**Kompetenzniveaustufe 3**
Inhaltliche und formale Textgestaltung (Vollständigkeit, Richtigkeit, Eigenständigkeit, Adressatenorientierung und Textformat)	Der Text enthält zwar einzelne Aspekte über das Leben der zu beschreibenden Person, aber es fehlen doch wesentliche Informationen. Er besteht aus nur wenigen Sätzen. Die Informationen sind zum größten Teil nicht strukturiert dargestellt, und der Einleitungssatz stellt die Person nicht richtig vor (oder fehlt ganz). Der Hauptteil ist sehr knapp und gibt kaum Detailinformationen. Insgesamt ist der Text nicht durch Absätze strukturiert.	Der Text gibt einen grundlegenden Überblick über das Leben der zu beschreibenden Person. Er gibt die wichtigsten Aspekte in Kürze wieder. Die Informationen sind zum Teil strukturiert dargestellt, und der Einleitungssatz stellt die Person grundlegend vor. Im Hauptteil werden nur wenige Detailinformationen gegeben. Insgesamt ist der Text zumindest teilweise durch Absätze strukturiert.	Der Text gibt einen guten Überblick über das Leben der zu beschreibenden Person. Er beinhaltet fast alle wichtigen Aspekte, meist in angemessenem Umfang. Die Informationen sind zum größten Teil strukturiert dargestellt, und der Einleitungssatz stellt die Person weitgehend angemessen vor. Im Hauptteil werden auch einige Detailinformationen gegeben. Insgesamt ist der Text durch Absätze strukturiert.
Empfohlener Übungsbereich	Übungsbereich 1: Inhaltliche Textgestaltung	Übungsbereich 2: Inhaltliche Textgestaltung	Übungsbereich 3: Inhaltliche Textgestaltung
Sprachliche Textgestaltung (Wortschatz, Grammatik und Orthografie)	Der Schreiber/Die Schreiberin verfügt über einen sehr eingeschränkten Grundwortschatz, es kommen häufig elementare Fehler und Wortwiederholungen vor. *Linking words* fehlen (fast) vollständig. Der Schreiber/Die Schreiberin verwendet zwar nicht immer vollständige Sätze, dennoch ist der Text auch für einen *Native Speaker* im Großen und Ganzen verständlich. Bei der Verwendung der Tempora *(past, present, future)* und Adjektiv/Adverb bestehen noch große Unsicherheiten in der Bildung und Anwendung. Auch bei der Einhaltung der *word order* zeigen sich noch beträchtliche Schwierigkeiten. Insgesamt kommen noch häufig elementare Grammatikfehler vor. Der Schreiber/Die Schreiberin beachtet kaum die Regeln der Orthografie.	Der Schreiber/Die Schreiberin kann den Grundwortschatz zumindest grundlegend anwenden, es kommen aber noch elementare Fehler und Wortwiederholungen vor. *Linking words* werden zum Teil eingebracht. Der Schreiber/Die Schreiberin verwendet weitgehend vollständige Sätze, die auch für einen *Native Speaker* weitgehend verständlich sind. Bei der Verwendung der Tempora *(past, present, future)* und Adjektiv/Adverb kommen noch Fehler bei der Bildung und/oder Anwendung vor. Auch die *word order* ist zum Teil noch fehlerhaft. Insgesamt kommen noch elementare Grammatikfehler vor. Der Schreiber/Die Schreiberin verstößt noch häufig gegen die Regeln der Orthografie.	Der Schreiber/Die Schreiberin kann den Grundwortschatz weitgehend sicher und abwechslungsreich anwenden, es kommen aber noch gelegentlich Fehler und Wortwiederholungen vor. *Linking words* werden häufiger eingebracht. Der Schreiber/Die Schreiberin verwendet fast durchgehend vollständige Sätze, die auch für einen *Native Speaker* verständlich sind. Bei der Verwendung der Tempora *(past, present, future)* und Adjektiv/Adverb kommen nur noch gelegentlich Fehler bei der Bildung und/oder Anwendung vor. Auch im Bereich *word order* zeigen sich noch kleinere Schwierigkeiten. Insgesamt kommen noch gelegentlich elementare Grammatikfehler vor. Der Schreiber/Die Schreiberin verstößt gelegentlich gegen die Regeln der Orthografie.
Empfohlener Übungsbereich	Übungsbereich 1: Sprachliche Textgestaltung	Übungsbereich 2: Sprachliche Textgestaltung	Übungsbereich 3: Sprachliche Textgestaltung

Teil 1: Inhaltliche Textgestaltung

Writing a short biography

Andreas and Dustin are basketball fans and they want to make a presentation about Kobe Bryant in their next English lesson. Help them to write a short biography by connecting the sentence halves.

> **Tipp**
>
> *Beginne mit einer allgemeinen Einleitung und Informationen zum Privatleben (Geburtstag, Eltern usw.). Berichte dann über Kobe Bryants Karriere und erwähne die wichtigen Ereignisse in chronologischer Reihenfolge. Beende deinen Text mit einem passenden Schlusssatz.*

Kobe Bryant

Match the sentence halves.

1. Kobe Bryant is one of the	_____	who played for the Philadelphia 76ers from 1975 to 1979.
2. He was born on	_____	best basketball players in the NBA.
3. His father is Joe Bryant	_____	brother was also a well-known NBA player.
4. His mother is Pamela Cox and her	_____	School near Philadelphia.
5. Kobe grew up in Italy	_____	August 23rd, 1978 in Philadelphia, Pennsylvania.
6. After their retrun to the USA, Kobe went to Lower Merion High	_____	and the second daughter followed only three years later.
7. He married his wife	_____	for the Charlotte Hornets.
8. In 2003 their first daughter was born	_____	and has played for them ever since.
10. When he was 18 he played	_____	and he even became the most valuable player in 2008.
11. After that he joined the Los Angeles Lakers in 1996	_____	because his father played for Italian clubs.
12. There he is having a successful time	_____	Vanessa in April 2001.

Now write the biography. Start a paragraph for each new idea.

Kobe Bryant is one of ______________________________

____

____

____

____

____

____

____

____

Teil 2: Sprachliche Textgestaltung

Working with words

Hier wiederholst du Begriffe und Wendungen, die wichtig sind, wenn du einen Text über eine berühmte Person schreiben möchtest.

1. Finding the right words

be born
marry ★ ~~boring~~
buy ★ ~~castle~~ ★ cinema
concert ★ daughter
famous ★ father
match ★ start

Find the right word in the star:

queen – *castle*

singer – ____________________

actor – ____________________

football player – ____________________

Find opposites in the star:

interesting – *boring*

sell – ____________________

die – ____________________

be divorced – ____________________

not known – ____________________

end – ____________________

son – ____________________

mother – ____________________

2. Tiger Woods

Can you put the letters into the right order?

> **Tipp** *Wenn es dir schwerfällt, die Buchstaben in die richtige Reihenfolge zu bringen, können dir vielleicht die Wörter in Aufgabe 1 helfen.*

Eldrick "Tiger" Woods is one of the most ______________ *(luscsucfes)* golf ______________ *(srapley)* in the history of sports. He is also one of the richest sportsmen.

Eldrick Woods was ______________ *(norb)* in Cypress/California on 30th December 1975 and soon after his birth one of his father's friends gave him the nickname "Tiger". Woods ______________ *(wreg)* up near Los Angeles. When he went to the kindergarten he got his first golf lesson. At the age of eight he ______________ *(now)* the Junior World Golf Championship. In the following years he won many other golf tournaments* for children and teenagers. In August 1996 he ________________ *(trasted)* his ________________ *(ercera)* as a professional golf player. In the same year he became "Sportsman of the Year", a title from an American sports magazine. In 1997 he won the US-Masters and became the ________________________________ *(bumner neo)* on the world ranking list**. He has won 88 tournaments so far and is still one of the best – if not the best – golf players in the world.

In October 2004 Tiger Woods ________________ *(riedmar)* the ex-model Elin Nordegren, they've got a ________________ *(uahgdert)* (Sam Alexis, 2007) and a ________________ *(ons)* (Charlie Axel, 2009).

Today Tiger Woods ________________ *(viles)* in Orlando/Florida with his ________________ *(mifaly)*.

*tournament = Turnier **world ranking list = Weltrangliste

Finding mistakes in a text

Hier lernst du, typische Rechtschreibfehler in einem Text zu finden und diese zu verbessern.
Beachte die Hinweise in dem Kasten.

Correcting a biography

Read the biography and underline the eight spelling mistakes.

William Bradley „Brad" Pitt

Brad Pitt was born on 18th december, 1963 in Shawnee, Oklahoma. When he was a child, he sang in a choir of a church. He is an american actor and producer. His family came from england.

Pitt attended Kickapoo High School, where he was a member of the golf, tennis and swiming team. In 1982 he went to Columbia Missourian School. The first greater film in his carreer was *Thelma and Louise.*

In 2000 he marryed Jennifer Aniston. His partner today is Angelina Jolie. He met her in the film *Mr and Mrs Smith*. Among Brads' most successfull films are *Troy* and *Ocean's Eleven, Twelve* and *Thirteen*.

Häufige Fehlerquellen

- Im Englischen werden Wochentage, Monatsnamen, Eigennamen, Länder und Nationalitäten immer großgeschrieben, z. B.: *Germany, January, Friday*.
- Manchmal ändert sich die Schreibweise, wenn ein Wort eine Endung erhält, z. B.: *try – tried* (aber: *play – played*), *run – running, take – taking, happy – happily.*
- Beachte: Wenn *full* ein eigenes Wort ist, schreibt man es mit zwei ‚l', als Anhängsel an ein anderes Wort aber nur mit einem ‚l', z. B.: *wonderful, beautiful.*
- Manchmal wird ein verwandtes Wort im Deutschen anders geschrieben als im Englischen.
- Achte darauf, dass der Apostroph an der richtigen Stelle steht: *the boy's father* (ein Junge), aber *the boys' father* (mehrere Jungen); ohne Apostroph: *the boys are at home* (mehrere Jungen).

Ordne die Fehler, die du gefunden hast, nun einer häufigen Fehlerquelle zu und vervollständige die Tabelle.

Groß-/Kleinschreibung	Fehler	Korrektur
Endung	**Fehler**	**Korrektur**
marryed	*y wird zu i*	*married*
full/-ful	**Fehler**	**Korrektur**
Unterschiede Deutsch – Englisch	**Fehler**	**Korrektur**
's, s' oder ohne Apostroph	**Fehler**	**Korrektur**

Now write down the correct text.

Teil 1: Inhaltliche Textgestaltung

Writing a short biography

Annika and Maike want to make a presentation about Michelle Obama in their next English lesson. Maike has already started some sentences for a biography. Annika has got a fact file about Michelle Obama. Help Maike and Annika to write a text.

Tipp *Beginne deinen Text mit einer allgemeinen Aussage über die Persönlichkeit, über die du schreibst. Vielen Lesern ist sie vielleicht noch gar nicht bekannt.*

Michelle Obama
Michelle Obama was born on ...
Her parents ...
She married ...
Michelle was an excellent student.
She went to ...
She left school ...
After school she ...
At first she studied ...
Later ...
There she ...
Her first job ...
Then she ...
Today she ...

Fact file

Full name	Michelle LaVaughn Robinson Obama
Place of birth	Chicago, Illinois
Date of birth	January 17th, 1964
Father	Frasier Robinson, engineer
Mother	Marian Robinson, secretary
School	Whitney Young Magnet High School (till 1981), excellent student
University	– Social Economics at Princeton University – Law at Harvard University till 1988 – became a Doctor Juris
Family status	married (husband US President Barack Obama, since October 1992, two daughters)
Career	– worked as a lawyer in Chicago – vice president at the University of Chicago – today she supports her husband

Now write the complete text. Start a paragraph for each major point: family, school, career, etc.

Das solltest du beim Schreiben einer Biografie beachten:

- Teile deinem Leser mit, um wen es geht und was ihn oder sie berühmt gemacht hat. Denke immer daran, dass nicht jeder ihn oder sie kennt.
- Beginne zunächst mit persönlichen Informationen (Geburtsdatum/-ort, Familie, Schule ...).
- Gib danach Informationen über den Verlauf der Karriere.
- Achte darauf, dass du deine Leser immer über die Familie, Schulzeit, den Karriereverlauf, den ersten/größten/letzten Erfolg informierst.

Teil 2: Sprachliche Textgestaltung

Working with words
Hier wiederholst du Begriffe und Wendungen, die wichtig sind, wenn du einen Text über eine berühmte Person schreiben möchtest.

Kate Hudson
Can you complete the words in the star? Fill in a, e, i, o or u.

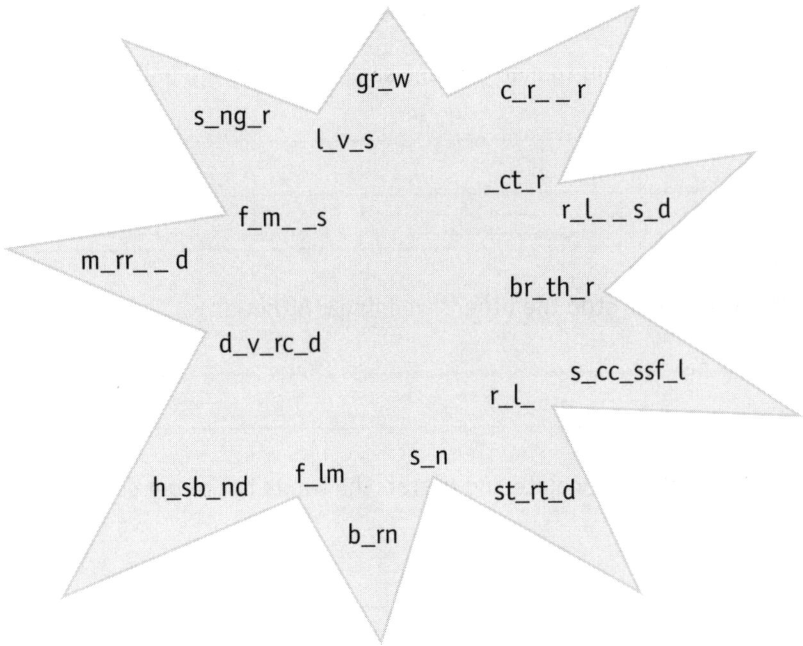

Now complete the text with the words in the star.

American actress Kate Hudson was ________________ in Los Angeles/California on 19th April 1979.
She ________________ up in the ________________ business as her mother is the ________________ actress Goldie Hawn. Her older ________________ Oliver is also an ________________.
She wasn't even three years old when her parents got ________________. But soon her mother had a new ________________, actor Kurt Russell, who became Kate's step-father.
When she was 17 she was a guest in the TV series *Party of Five,* but her ________________ really ________________ with the film *Almost famous* in 2000. She was even nominated for her small ________________ for the Golden Globe and the Oscar. After that she had many other ________________ films like *How to lose a guy in 10 days, Raising Helen, Fool's Gold.* Her new film *Bride Wars* will be ________________ soon.
When she was 21, she ________________ rock ________________ Chris Robinson, who is the father of her ________________. But after six years they got divorced. Now she ________________ with actor Owen Wilson.

Using linking words

Hier übst du, Sätze miteinander zu verknüpfen.

Bride Wars

Connect the sentences with the words in brackets.

a) Kate Hudson's new film *Bride Wars* is about two friends. The film will be released soon. (which)

Kate Hudson's new film Bride Wars, which will be ______________________

____

b) Liv and Emma find out that they plan to marry on the same day. They are both very angry. (When)

____

____

____

c) They are good friends. They try to stop the other's wedding. (Although)

____

____

d) One friend gives the other lots of chocolate and butter. She wants her to get so fat that she doesn't fit into her wedding dress. (because)

____

____

____

e) Liv exchanges a DVD. Emma wants to show the DVD at her wedding. Later she feels bad about it. She tries to put the right DVD back. (which, but, and)

____

____

____

f) There will be only one wedding on this day. Both will be happy in the end. (although)

____

____

Finding mistakes in a text

Hier lernst du, typische Rechtschreib-, Zeiten- und Wortstellungsfehler in einem Text zu finden und diese zu verbessern. Beachte die Hinweise in dem Kasten.

Correcting a biography

Read the biography and underline the eleven mistakes.

Miley Cyrus

Miley Cyrus is a very succesfull american singer, actress and author. Miley Cyrus is born on november 23rd, 1992 in Nashville, Tennessee.
She acts as Hannah Montana since 2006.
Mileys parents are Leticia „Tish" and Billy Ray Cyrus, who is a country singer. She has got three brothers and sisters. Some of them are artists too.
In 2003 played she "Young Ruthie" in Tim Burton's *Big Fish*. This was her first film role and her first CD album followed only three years later. In October 2006 sang she eight songs from the Hannah Montana show for her first CD.
Miley is singel and she says she is loveing it, because life is so carefree. Despite of this is she a very responsible person, who cares for other people.

- Tipps zur Rechtschreibung findest du auf S. 51.
- Satzbau: Das Subjekt des Satzes steht immer vor dem Verb.
- Zeiten: Nach Zeitangaben der Vergangenheit steht das *simple past*. *For/since* steht mit dem *present perfect*.

Ordne die Fehler nun der richtigen Gruppe zu und trage sie in die Tabelle ein.

Rechtschreibung	Fehler	Korrektur
american	Nationalitäten werden großgeschrieben	American
Zeiten	Fehler	Korrektur
Satzbau	Fehler	Korrektur

Now write down the correct text in your exercise book. You can add some more information if you want to.

Teil 1: Inhaltliche Textgestaltung

Writing a biography

Your English teacher wants you to write a biography of your favourite star. Now choose a star and find information about him or her. Write the biography in your exercise book.

Tipp *Beachte beim Schreiben der Biografie die Hinweise in dem Kasten und hake die erledigten Punkte ab.*

Tips for writing a good biography

Always follow these three steps: pre-, while- and post-writing.

1. Pre-writing

☐ Collect information about the following points:
- When and where was your star born?
- What do you know about his or her family?
- What can you tell about his or her school days/time at university?
- When did he or she make the first film/CD/big match/...?
- What was his or her last success?
- How did he or she become famous?

☐ Organize the information (use one of the following two methods).
- Draw a mind map.

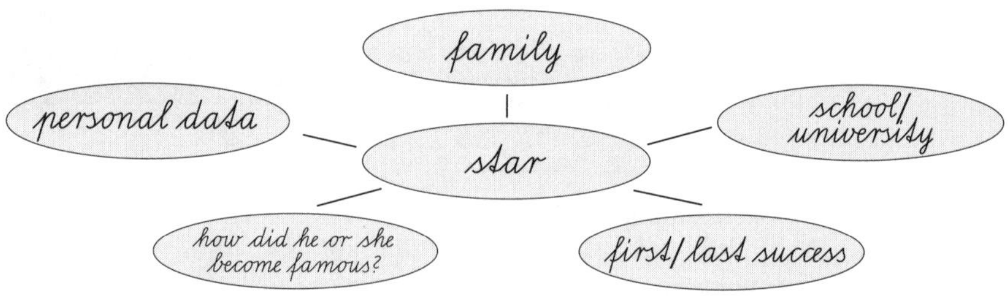

- Arrange the information in a chart.

Personal data	Family	School/university	How did he or she become famous?	First/last success

2. While-writing

☐ Tell the reader at the beginning who the biography is about.
☐ Give some general information about your star. Perhaps not everybody knows him or her.
☐ Give the personal information first.
☐ Then give necessary details about the career.
☐ Make paragraphs for new ideas (e.g. family, school, career, ...).
☐ Make sure that you include the important facts of your chart or mind map.

3. Post-writing

Before you present the biography to your class, you should read it several times and answer the following questions:

☐ Is the biography complete? Are there answers to all important questions?
☐ Does the reader get a quick information about the star?
☐ Does the biography have uninteresting details about the star? If so, delete them.
☐ Check your biography carefully for mistakes.

Tipp: Make a personal checklist with your most common mistakes and use it for revising your reports.

Teil 2: Sprachliche Textgestaltung

Working with words

Hier wiederholst du Begriffe und Wendungen, die wichtig sind, wenn du einen Text über eine berühmte Person schreiben möchtest.

Michael Jackson

Tick the right words or phrases.

> **Tipp**
> *Lies dir die möglichen Antworten sehr genau durch, denn oft unterscheiden sie sich nur in einzelnen Buchstaben. Wenn du bei einer Aufgabe die Antwort nicht weißt, versuche schon einmal, die Antworten zu streichen, die auf gar keinen Fall infrage kommen. Dadurch bleiben weniger Antworten übrig, und dann fällt es dir vielleicht leichter, die richtige herauszufinden.*

1. Michael Jackson is one of the most famous stars in the history of pop music. He …
- ☐ **a)** … was born on 29th August 1958 in Gary/Indiana.
- ☐ **b)** … was born in Gary/Indiana on 29th August 1958.
- ☐ **c)** … was burn on 29th August 1958 in Gary/Indiana.
- ☐ **d)** … was burn in Gary/Indiana on 29th August 1958.

2. He … in a big family with six brothers and three sisters.
- ☐ **a)** … lifed …
- ☐ **b)** … lift …
- ☐ **c)** … lives …
- ☐ **d)** … lived …

3. His … with his band Jackson Five, which he formed together with his brothers Jackie, Tito, Jermaine and Marlon in 1965.
- ☐ **a)** … career started …
- ☐ **b)** … carreer started …
- ☐ **c)** … carer started …
- ☐ **d)** … career stated …

4. The Jackson Five soon …
- ☐ **a)** … became famos.
- ☐ **b)** … became famous.
- ☐ **c)** … become famos.
- ☐ **d)** … become famous.

5. … 1971 he started his solo career, although he was only 13 years old.
- ☐ **a)** At …
- ☐ **b)** On …
- ☐ **c)** In …
- ☐ **d)** Of …

6. When he released his first solo-album, it soon became quite …
- ☐ **a)** … successful
- ☐ **b)** … sucessful
- ☐ **c)** … successfull
- ☐ **d)** … sucessfull

7. On 1st December 1982 he released his album *Thriller* which soon became a …
- ☐ **a)** … nomber one hit.
- ☐ **b)** … nomber one hitt.
- ☐ **c)** … number one hit.
- ☐ **d)** … number one hitt.

8. Many successful hits followed and so people … him King of Pop.
- ☐ **a)** … caught …
- ☐ **b)** … cold …
- ☐ **c)** … called …
- ☐ **d)** … colled …

9. From 1994 to 1995 he was … to Lisa Marie Presley and from 1996 to 1999 to Deborah Jeanne Rowe, who became the mother of his two …
- ☐ **a)** … married … children.
- ☐ **b)** … married … childs.
- ☐ **c)** … maried … children.
- ☐ **d)** … maried … childs.

10. Michael Jackson … in Los Angeles on 25th June 2009.
- ☐ **a)** … dead …
- ☐ **b)** … dad …
- ☐ **c)** … died …
- ☐ **d)** … death …

Using linking words

Hier übst du, Sätze miteinander zu verknüpfen.

The King of Pop

Can you connect the following sentences?

a) Michael Jackson became the star of the Jackson Five. He was only a little boy.

b) He was 13 years old. He started his solo career.

c) Michael Jackson's *Thriller* is one of the most successful albums in the world. It was sold 109 million times.

d) His marriage with Lisa Marie Presley was not very happy. They got divorced.

e) He had had many other successful albums like *Bad* and *Invincible*. He won a Bambi as the greatest living pop icon.

f) People called him the King of Pop. He was very successful and had so many fans.

g) He grew up in a big family. He had many fans. He was very lonely.

h) He died. He was 50 years old.

Finding mistakes in a text

Hier übst du, typische Rechtschreib-, Zeiten- und Wortstellungsfehler in einem Text zu finden und diese zu verbessern.

Correcting a biography

Read the biography and find eighteen mistakes.

Beyoncé Knowles

Beyoncé Knowles is a very succesfull american singer, actress and author. She is born on september 4th, 1981 in Houston, Texas. In the late 1990s was she the lead singer of Destinys Child. The band sold more than 50 million albums since then.

Beyoncé started singing and dancing when she was very young. She won her first contest in 1988 in Texas, where she went to school. This realy was the start of a great carreer. In 1997 recorded her group Destiny's Child the soundtrack for the film *Men in Black*.

In June 2003 released she her debut solo album, *Dangerously in Love*. She was awarded five Grammys for this album in 2004. Her most popular hit is *If I were a boy* which was released in 2008. She is not only known as a singer but also as an actress. She started her acting career in 2001. Her first film was *Carmen: A Hip Hopera*. Later was she Steve Martins film partner in *The Pink Panther*.

At April 4th, 2008 she marryed the rapper Jay-Z who had already been her partner for more than six years. One of the biggest events in her life was definitely her appearance at Barack Obamas presidential party on January 20th, 2009, when she sang a song for the first dance of the new President and First Lady.

Mistake	Correction	Mistake	Correction

Now write the correct text in your exercise book. You may add some more information if you want to.

Übungsbereich 1

Writing a short biography

Kobe Bryant is one of the best basketball players in the NBA. He was born on August 23rd, 1978 in Philadelphia, Pennsylvania. His father is Joe Bryant who played for the Philadelphia 76ers from 1975 to 1979. His mother is Pamela Cox and her brother was also a well-known NBA player. Kobe grew up in Italy because his father played for Italian clubs. After their return to the USA, Kobe went to Lower Merion High School near Philadelphia. He married his wife Vanessa in April 2001. In 2003 their first daughter was born and the second daughter followed only three years later. When he was 18 he played for the Charlotte Hornets. After that he joined the Los Angeles Lakers in 1996 and has played for them ever since. There he is having a successful time and he even became the most valuable player in 2008.

Working with words

1. Finding the right words

singer – concert, actor – cinema, football player – match

sell – buy, die – be born, be divorced – marry, not known – famous, end – start, son – father/daughter, mother – daughter/father

2. Tiger Woods

successful, players, born, grew, won, started, career, number one, married, daughter, son, lives, family

Finding mistakes in a text

William Bradley „Brad" Pitt

Brad Pitt was born on 18th December, 1963 in Shawnee, Oklahoma. When he was a child, he sang in a choir of a church. He is an American actor and producer. His family came from England.

Pitt attended Kickapoo High School, where he was a member of the golf, tennis and swimming team.

In 1982 he went to Columbia Missourian School.

The first greater film in his career was *Thelma and Louise.*

In 2000 he married Jennifer Aniston. His partner today is Angelina Jolie. He met her in the film *Mr and Mrs Smith*. Among Brad's most successful films are *Troy* and *Ocean's Eleven, Twelve* and *Thirteen.*

Übungsbereich 2

Writing a short biography

The US President's wife Michelle Obama was born on January 17th, 1964 in Chicago, Illinois. Her parents are Frasier and Marian Robinson. Her father is an engineer and her mother a secretary.

She married Barack Obama in October 1992.

They have two daughters.

Michelle was an excellent student.

She went to Whitney Young Magnet High School.

She left school in 1981. After school she went to university. At first she studied Social Economics at Princeton University. Later she studied Law at Harvard University. There she became a Doctor Juris.

Her first job was in Chicago. She worked as a lawyer.

Then she was a vice president at the University of Chicago. Today she supports her husband.

Working with words

born, grew, film, famous, brother, actor, divorced, husband, career, started, role, successful, released, married, singer, son, lives

Using linking words

a) Kate Hudson's new film *Bride Wars,* which will be released soon, is about two friends.

b) When Liv and Emma find out that they plan to marry on the same day, they are both very angry.

c) Although they are good friends, they try to stop the other's wedding.

d) One friend gives the other lots of chocolate and butter because she wants her to get so fat that she doesn't fit into her wedding dress.

e) Liv exchanges a DVD which Emma wants to show at her wedding, but later she feels bad about it and tries to put the right DVD back.

f) Although there will be only one wedding on this day, both will be happy in the end.

Finding mistakes in a text
Miley Cyrus
Miley Cyrus is a very succesful American singer, actress author. Miley Cyrus was born on November 23rd, 1992 in Nashville, Tennessee. She has acted as Hannah Montana since 2006. Miley's parents are Leticia „Tish" and Billy Ray Cyrus, who is a country singer. She has got three brothers and sisters. Some of them are artists too.
In 2003 she played „Young Ruthie" in Tim Burton's *Big Fish*. This was her first film role and her first CD album followed only three years later. In October 2006 she sang eight songs from the Hannah Montana show for her first CD.
Miley is single and she says she loves it, because life is so carefree. Despite of this she is a very responsible person, who cares for other people.

Übungsbereich 3

Writing a biography
Individuelle Lösungen

Working with words
1b, 2d, 3a, 4b, 5c, 6a, 7c, 8c, 9a, 10a

Using linking words
Individuelle Schülerlösungen, zum Beispiel:

a) Michael Jackson became the star of the Jackson Five although/but he was only a little boy.
b) When he was 13 years old, he started his solo career.
c) Michael Jackson's *Thriller*, which was sold 109 million times, is one of the most successful albums in the world./Michael Jackson's *Thriller* is one of the most successful albums in the world, because it was sold 109 million times.
d) His marriage with Lisa Marie Presley was not very happy, so they got divorced.
e) After he had had many other successful albums like *Bad* and *Invincible*, he won a Bambi as the greatest living pop icon.
f) People called him the King of Pop, because he was very successful and had so many fans.
g) He grew up in a big family and had many fans, but he was very lonely./Although he grew up in a big family and had many fans, he was very lonely.
h) He died when he was 50 years old.

Finding mistakes in a text
Beyoncé Knowles
Beyoncé Knowles is a very succesful American singer, actress and author. She was born on September 4th, 1981 in Houston, Texas. In the late 1990s she was the lead singer of Destiny's Child. The band has sold more than 50 million albums since then.
Beyoncé started singing and dancing when she was very young. She won her first contest in Texas in 1988, where she went to school. This really was the start of a great career. In 1997 her group Destiny's Child recorded the soundtrack for the film *Men in Black*.
In June 2003 she released her debut solo album, *Dangerously in Love*. She was awarded five Grammies for this album in 2004. Her most popular hit is *If I were a boy* which was released in 2008. She is not only known as a singer but also as an actress. She started her acting career in 2001. Her first film was *Carmen: A Hip Hopera*. Later she was Steve Martin's film partner in *The Pink Panther*.
On April 4th, 2008 she married the rapper Jay-Z who had already been her partner for more than six years. One of the biggest events in her life was definitely her appearance at Barack Obama's presidential party on January 20th, 2009, when she sang a song for the first dance of the new President and First Lady.

LERNFORTSCHRITTSERMITTLUNG: BIOGRAPHY

Name: ______________________ Class: __________ Date: ____________

Write a biography of 120 – 150 words about a famous person (an actress/actor, a singer, a sportswoman/-man, a writer, a politician, a scientist).

You should write about:
- when and where the famous person was born
- his or her family
- how his or her career began
- why people know him or her
- what his or her first great success was
- ...